Union Public Library
1980 Morris Avenue
Union, N.J. 07083

W9-AES-475

Lady Gaga

by Claire Kreger-Boaz

Union Public Library
1980 Morris Avenue
Union, N.J. 07083

LUCENT BOOKS

A part of Gale, Cengage Learning

GALE
CENGAGE Learning

Detroit • New York • San Francisco • New Haven, Conn • Waterville, Maine • London

© 2011 Gale, Cengage Learning

ALL RIGHTS RESERVED. No part of this work covered by the copyright herein may be reproduced, transmitted, stored, or used in any form or by any means graphic, electronic, or mechanical, including but not limited to photocopying, recording, scanning, digitizing, taping, Web distribution, information networks, or information storage and retrieval systems, except as permitted under Section 107 or 108 of the 1976 United States Copyright Act, without the prior written permission of the publisher.

Every effort has been made to trace the owners of copyrighted material.

LIBRARY OF CONGRESS CATALOGING-IN-PUBLICATION DATA

Boaz, Claire Kreger, 1973-
  Lady Gaga / by Claire Kreger-Boaz.
    p. cm. -- (People in the news)
  Includes bibliographical references and index.
  ISBN 978-1-4205-0426-2 (hardcover)
  1. Lady Gaga--Juvenile literature. 2. Singers--United States--Biography--Juvenile literature. I. Title.
  ML3930.L13B62 2011
  782.42164092--dc22
  [B]

2010045426

Lucent Books
27500 Drake Rd.
Farmington Hills, MI 48331

ISBN-13: 978-1-4205-0426-2
ISBN-10: 1-4205-0426-6

Printed in the United States of America
1 2 3 4 5 6 7 15 14 13 12 11
Printed by Bang Printing, Brainerd, MN, 1st Ptg.,04/2011

Contents

Foreword

F ame and celebrity are alluring. People are drawn to those who walk in fame's spotlight, whether they are known for great accomplishments or for notorious deeds. The lives of the famous pique public interest and attract attention, perhaps because their experiences seem in some ways so different from, yet in other ways so similar to, our own.

Newspapers, magazines, and television regularly capitalize on this fascination with celebrity by running profiles of famous people. For example, television programs such as *Entertainment Tonight* devote all of their programming to stories about entertainment and entertainers. Magazines such as *People* fill their pages with stories of the private lives of famous people. Even newspapers, newsmagazines, and television news frequently delve into the lives of well-known personalities. Despite the number of articles and programs, few provide more than a superficial glimpse at their subjects.

Lucent's People in the News series offers young readers a deeper look into the lives of today's newsmakers, the influences that have shaped them, and the impact they have had in their fields of endeavor and on other people's lives. The subjects of the series hail from many disciplines and walks of life. They include authors, musicians, athletes, political leaders, entertainers, entrepreneurs, and others who have made a mark on modern life and who, in many cases, will continue to do so for years to come.

These biographies are more than factual chronicles. Each book emphasizes the contributions, accomplishments, or deeds that have brought fame or notoriety to the individual and shows how that person has influenced modern life. Authors portray their subjects in a realistic, unsentimental light. For example, Bill Gates—the cofounder and chief executive officer of the software giant Microsoft—has been instrumental in making personal computers the most vital tool of the modern age. Few dispute his business savvy, his perseverance, or his technical

4

expertise, yet critics say he is ruthless in his dealings with competitors and driven more by his desire to maintain Microsoft's dominance in the computer industry than by an interest in furthering technology.

In these books, young readers will encounter inspiring stories about real people who achieved success despite enormous obstacles. Oprah Winfrey—the most powerful, most watched, and wealthiest woman on television today—spent the first six years of her life in the care of her grandparents while her unwed mother sought work and a better life elsewhere. Her adolescence was colored by pregnancy at age fourteen, rape, and sexual abuse.

Each author documents and supports his or her work with an array of primary and secondary source quotations taken from diaries, letters, speeches, and interviews. All quotes are footnoted to show readers exactly how and where biographers derive their information and provide guidance for further research. The quotations enliven the text by giving readers eyewitness views of the life and accomplishments of each person covered in the People in the News series.

In addition, each book in the series includes photographs, annotated bibliographies, timelines, and comprehensive indexes. For both the casual reader and the student researcher, the People in the News series offers insight into the lives of today's newsmakers—people who shape the way we live, work, and play in the modern age.

A Glorious Reality Based on Beautiful Lies

During a performance at the Verizon Center in Washington, D.C., on September 7, 2010, Lady Gaga stopped singing her hit single, "Just Dance," to break up a fistfight between two fans in the front row. She ordered her dancers and the music to stop, and the sold-out venue, which holds more than twenty thousand people, gave Gaga its full attention.

She walked toward the fighting fans and told them her show was not a place to fight, but rather an opportunity to experience joy and happiness. She said that "only fake monster fighting" was allowed. The crowd cheered and screamed in agreement. Gaga then asked the crowd, "Does everyone know what I hate more than anything? I hate the truth! In fact, I hate the truth so much I prefer giant doses of bull-[expletive] any day!"[1]

This call to embrace theatrical exaggeration is central to the Gaga experience. Known as "Mother Monster" to her devoted fans, whom she calls her "Little Monsters," Lady Gaga wants to manufacture an atmosphere of fun, love, and happiness that is so transcendent that the audience forgets all of the things they do not like about themselves and each other. She wants her fans to be transformed by the temporary reality she constructs for them. In short, Lady Gaga wants to create a new reality based on a beautiful lie.

"I Hate the Truth!"

In the interlude during her concerts, Lady Gaga celebrates her fans with a short movie called the *Monster Film*, in which Gaga reads from her "Manifesto of Little Monsters," a love letter to her fans that is included in the Super Deluxe edition of her album, *The Fame Monster*. Gaga reads the following message as the movie is projected on giant screens: "It is in the theory of perception that we have established our bond. Or, the lie, I should say, for which we kill. We are nothing without our image. Without our projection. Without the spiritual hologram of who we perceive ourselves to be, or to become rather, in the future. When you're lonely, I'll be lonely too. And this is *The Fame*."[2] During her performances, Lady Gaga urges her fans to forget their real lives and accept and share the reality she creates for them. In Gaga's world, no one is fat, ugly, or alone, and there are no losers. According to Gaga, everyone is beautiful, and anyone can be famous.

In order to claim "the fame," however, one must be willing to forget about the truth. Gaga screams, "I hate the truth!" during her concerts as she demands that her audience to join her on a shared journey toward emancipation from self-doubt and fear. As Gaga explained her goal in an interview with *Rolling Stone*, "I want people to walk around delusional about how great they can be—and then to fight so hard for it every day that the lie becomes the truth."[3]

Gaga embodies this rule and is herself a walking contradiction. She is at once primal and technological, sophisticated and basic, intimate and exhibitionistic. She is above all committed to creating a glorious artificiality, a beautiful lie. She invites her audience to share in the moment to whatever degree they can participate. Journalist Jon Caramanica wrote of Gaga's world, "In her somewhat un-meticulously constructed universe, there's nothing that can't be rewritten, refigured, revised or reborn."[4] Indeed, for two-plus hours, Lady Gaga begs her fans to believe that anything is possible and that truth is merely a collective agreement to enjoy an experience.

Mother of Reinvention

What sets Lady Gaga apart from other performers is that her commitment to creating a particular experience and to altering her fans' reality is not just the goal of her tour. It is also how she lives her life. Gaga works tirelessly on her art. Her desire to shock and create through new songs, videos, technological gadgets, and fashion statements is born out of a seemingly compulsive need to express what she calls "the fame." In fact, Gaga has said that she is a product of a force outside of herself. She said in one interview, "I didn't create the fame. The fame created me."[5]

Indeed, Lady Gaga is not a mere character she plays, but rather a comprehensive persona brought to life through sheer will and imagination. She is constantly under construction, and no final version of the megastar is as of yet in sight. Gaga uses artistic expression to create beautiful lies that both hide and expose ugly truths. She constantly plays reality-bending games to the point that no one really knows fact from fiction. One critic who wrote a satirical piece blasting Gaga noted that he was commenting on sound bytes that may not even be true. Said Rick Newman, "It's possible that the mischievous Gaga is fooling everybody by making random statements that don't reflect her true feelings. So maybe the joke is on me and my fellow scolds."[6]

In her live performances, Gaga uses a visual and sonic assault to annihilate the senses and break through the wall between audience and performer. Through her performances, her fashions, and the way she lives her life, Gaga teaches her fans that the truth is subject to interpretation. She leads by example with her almost pathological commitment to reinvention. She changes her story every day: She is gay, she is straight, she is bisexual; she is a woman, she is a man, she is a transvestite and a hermaphrodite; she is anything and everything all at once. Indeed, Lady Gaga will neither confirm nor deny the rumors, because for her, the truth is beside the point.

Her audiences claim that Lady Gaga sets herself apart from other performers by creating an experience and altering her audience's sense of reality.

Chapter 1

Life Before Gaga

Lady Gaga was born Stefani Joanne Angelina Germanotta on March 28, 1986, to Italian Americans Joseph and Cynthia Germanotta. Stefani's parents were Internet entrepreneurs who recognized the great potential of the World Wide Web before it went mainstream. Joseph was in charge of a company that installed Wi-Fi in trendy hotels, and Cynthia worked as a vice president at Verizon. The Germanottas' shrewd business sense earned them enough money to be considered upper-middle class. Thus, they were able to afford to live in the Upper West Side of New York City, a cultural mecca for music, dance, and theater.

Stefani and her younger sister, Natali, who was born on March 10, 1992, grew up surrounded by world-renowned performance venues. The Germanottas lived close to Central Park, near the Lincoln Center for the Performing Arts and the Beacon Theater. Joseph performed as a musician in the evenings, after work. He shared his love of music with young Stefani, and he often danced with her around the Germanotta duplex while listening to the Rolling Stones and the Beatles. When Stefani was just four years old, she wowed her family when she learned to play piano by ear. Stefani's parents encouraged her natural talent and paid for lessons throughout her childhood. Indeed, long before Stefani Germanotta became Lady Gaga, there were indications that she was gifted. She showed early talent in music and theater and a peculiar sensitivity that set her apart from her peers.

An Elite Education

Joseph and Cynthia sent their daughters to a prestigious, all-girl Catholic school, Convent of the Sacred Heart. Sacred Heart is located on Ninety-First Street, on the Upper West Side of New York City. It is across from the Guggenheim Museum in the heart of one of the city's wealthiest neighborhoods. The exclusive private school demands of its students a rigorous academic

Lady Gaga was born Stefani Germanotta on March 28, 1986, to parents Cynthia and Joseph Germanotta.

Convent of the Sacred Heart

The Convent of the Sacred Heart is New York City's oldest private school for girls. Founded in 1881, the school is located on Manhattan's Upper East Side in the former Otto Kahn and James A. Burden Jr. mansions, both of which are New York City–designated landmarks. Sacred Heart is an elite and expensive preparatory school. Annual tuition is over thirty-three thousand dollars. Notable alumnae include Caroline Kennedy, Gloria Vanderbilt, and Paris and Nicky Hilton. Lady Gaga's sister, Natali, graduated from the school in June 2010.

schedule, but the administration also enforces a performing arts curriculum that begins in kindergarten and continues through high school. Sacred Heart requires each student to enroll in at least two music or drama classes and to perform in at least two school productions per academic year. Once in high school, girls are offered the chance to audition for two full-scale musical productions per year.

Stefani played in her first piano recital at Sacred Heart when she was eight years old. She recalls the performance with affection and confidence: "I did a really good job. I was quite good."[7] In fact, Stefani was such a natural performer that her parents enrolled her in daylong acting classes on Saturdays when she was eleven years old. Stefani immediately excelled in her drama classes. She vividly remembers her first acting lesson, in which she was asked to pretend to drink a cup of coffee. She attributes her dramatic ability both to these early classes and a heightened "sense memory" that allows her to intimately feel what she is trying to portray. As she has put it, "I can feel the rain [even] when it's not raining."[8]

Beginning in eighth grade, Stefani performed in several musical theater productions. She landed the lead in nearly every play she auditioned for, including the lead role of Adelaide in *Guys and Dolls*. Fellow cast members recall that Stefani insisted that they call her by her character's name backstage and during rehearsals, which they found odd.

An Outcast from the Start

Many of the girls at Sacred Heart were jealous of Stefani's talent and overdeveloped physique. They came up with mean nicknames for her, such as "The Germ" and "Big Boobs McGee." Stefani's sexy style also proved too racy for the faculty, and her teachers frequently complained that her skirts were too short and her shirts were too tight. She argued that she dressed exactly the same as the other students, but notes that she was about 15 to 20 pounds (6.8 to 9 kg) heavier than most girls, which made her look more grown-up in the Catholic school uniforms. Stefani felt increasingly like an outcast, but refused to stifle her creative side just to fit in with her peers.

When she was fifteen years old, her oddball personality was enhanced by the September 11, 2001, terrorist attacks against the United States. After the World Trade Center towers fell, killing nearly three thousand Americans, she became morose and exceedingly dramatic. She showed up to school without makeup and wore black clothes in mourning. She cried openly and uncontrollably throughout the day. She even changed the way she walked, adopting a deliberate stomp. Stefani's peers had already considered her to be dramatic, dark, and strange, but her reaction to the 9/11 attacks made her even more of an outcast. As a result, she felt even further isolated. As she told Ellen DeGeneres in a 2009 interview, "I didn't fit in in high school and I felt like a freak."[9] One of the few places she felt comfortable was onstage, where she could express her creativity and lose herself in whichever character she played.

Musical Prodigy

Though she loved theater, music was Stefani's first love and the focus of her early arts education. She attributes her ability to write hit songs to the strict classical music training she received at Sacred Heart. "I was classically trained as a pianist and that innately teaches you how to write a pop song, because when you learn Bach inversions, it has the same sort of modulations between the chords," she says. "It's all about tension and release."[10] By the time she was thirteen years old, Stefani had written her first piano ballad, "To Love Again."

When she was fourteen years old, Stefani regularly showed up at open mike nights to play her songs in front of an audience at nightclubs around New York City. She was almost always accompanied by her mother, since she was too young to be admitted to the mostly twenty-one-and-up venues. Cynthia wholeheartedly supported her daughter; in fact, she believed so deeply in her talent that she would promise club managers they would not be disappointed if they let her perform.

Stefani was instantly hooked on playing music before an audience. It was as though she was born to perform. "I was always an entertainer. I was a ham as a little girl and I'm a ham today,"[11] she says. But the more she performed, the more she earned comparisons to female singer/songwriters such as Fiona Apple. Stefani did not care for this comparison, because she wanted to be seen as an original, a star. She sought to distinguish herself by expanding her act to play with a full rock band. Therefore, at sixteen, Stefani formed a classic rock cover band that performed her favorite songs. Thanks in part to her father's taste in music, Stefani's influences at the time included the Rolling Stones, Bruce Springsteen, Pink Floyd, Led Zeppelin, and the Beatles.

In addition to performing with her cover band, Stefani also worked on writing original ballads. In 2002 she recorded her first demo. She was proud of her songs, and her parents were so impressed that they gave the demo away as party favors at the "sweet sixteen" party they threw for her. Attendees were blown away by Stefani's recording and suspected she had the talent and persona to become a star.

Lady Gaga plays the piano in concert. She played her first recital at Sacred Heart when she was eight years old.

Work Hard, Play Hard

Stefani was not just a talented musician and actress, however. She was also a hard worker. In addition to writing and performing her music, starring in plays, and carrying her high school academic load, she worked part-time as a waitress in a diner. One reason she took a part-time job was to be able to afford the trendy purses and fashions that came so easily to her wealthier classmates. The Germanottas, though well off, were nowhere near as rich as some of Stefani's high-profile peers. Moreover, they refused to drop hundreds of dollars on a purse just to help their daughter fit in.

Another reason Stefani worked at the diner was so she could indulge her wild side without her parents' knowledge. For example, she used the money she made waiting tables to get her first tattoo—a G clef on her lower back—when she was seventeen years old. She also began to date a twenty-six-year-old waiter from the diner and went out to clubs on weekends, where she used a fake ID (which she purchased with her paycheck). Stefani knew her father would not approve of her antics, and her waitressing job was the only way she could get away with them. It served as her alibi and funded her bad-girl behaviors, and it also taught her how to be resourceful to get what she wanted on her own.

Gaga Goes to College

All of Stefani's talent and hard work paid off in 2003 when, at seventeen years old, she was one of twenty people in the world admitted to the Tisch School of the Arts at New York University. Tisch is a highly competitive conservatory that specializes in the study of theater, dance, and film. Some famous alumni include directors Oliver Stone and Martin Scorsese, as well as actors Angelina Jolie, Whoopi Goldberg, Debra Messing (*Will and Grace*), and Daniel Dae Kim (*Lost*).

At Tisch, Stefani studied music and drama and wrote critical essays about art, religion, and social justice. She learned how to think critically about art and music, and she worked furiously

The Art of Spencer Tunick and Damien Hirst

Spencer Tunick is an American photographer who specializes in installations of large groups of nude people posed in urban spaces (although he has shot nudes in forests and on beaches as well). Damien Hirst is a British artist whose art installations are often composed of dead animals preserved in formaldehyde and placed in vitrines, large glass display cases. Both artists challenge viewers by bringing intimately private subjects (nudity and death) into public space and by juxtaposing the organic with the artificial and the living with the inanimate. Their images are shocking and provocative, and simultaneously beautiful and disturbing. Stefani Germanotta was heavily influenced by the artistic styles of these two men.

Photographer Spencer Tunick stands next to one of his photos. Germanotta was heavily influenced by his art and that of Damien Hirst.

to hone her songwriting skills. She also wrote an eighty-page thesis on Spencer Tunick and Damien Hirst, two artists who deeply influenced her understanding of how to marry art with performance. Tunick documented in photographs and video large groups of people in the nude; Hirst created art out of dead animals. These graphic and shocking styles became ingrained in Stefani's consciousness and would later surface in her performance style.

Once Stefani learned to view art in a way that she found satisfying, she saw no further reason to go to college. She had already become frustrated with the critiques of her performances at Tisch. For example, when she did pop music and dance performances, she was told by her peers and teachers that she should do theater; but when she auditioned for musicals, she was criticized for being "too pop." After her second semester, she viewed studying performance as a waste of her talent and decided to quit Tisch to pursue her true passion: music.

As always, her parents were supportive of her decision. This time, however, there was a catch: If she did not succeed in music, she must agree to return to Tisch and finish her college degree. She agreed, and for one full year, her parents paid the rent on her apartment while she figured out what to do next.

On Her Own

While weighing her options and plotting her future, Stefani lived and worked out of her small Lower East Side apartment. She had one year to make it, or her parents would cut her off and force her to return to school. To support herself, she worked as a waitress at the Cornelia Street Café in Greenwich Village. The artsy café has a performance space downstairs that hosts the Songwriter's Exchange, a songwriting workshop of which Suzanne Vega is an alumna. She hung her favorite Yoko Ono record above her bed for inspiration. Of this time on her own, she says, "I didn't know somebody, who knew somebody, who knew somebody. If I have any advice to anybody, it's to just do it yourself, and don't waste time trying to get a favor."[12]

Stefani and her SGBand performed at many New York City nightclubs, including the Mercury Lounge.

During this time, she performed with her band, the SGBand (Stefani Germanotta Band) in several clubs around New York City, such as the Bitter End, the Mercury Lounge, and the Rockwood Music Hall. She relied on her creative instincts to get the SGBand gigs. For example, she pretended to be the SGBand's publicist, and as this character made phone calls to the booking agents at the clubs where she wanted to play. She pitched "her client" to them as if they were getting the inside scoop on the next big thing.

Kenny Gorka, a booking agent for the Bitter End at the time, still remembers Germanotta's call. "She lied to me, talking about how great Stephani [sic] was in the third person," he recalls. "But it was enough to pique my interest, and I brought her in for an audition and booked her."[13] The SGBand was getting gigs, and each performance seemed to bring Stefani Germanotta closer to becoming Lady Gaga.

The Emergence of Lady Gaga

G ermanotta's experience at Tisch left her dissatisfied and restless. She knew she would never return to New York University and that her parents would be disappointed. Still, she viewed college as a distraction that would delay the fame she felt destined to achieve. She wanted to live art, make music, and become a star, but she also had to support herself. It was during this time that she met people who would become instrumental in Stefani Germanotta's transformation into Lady Gaga—and to the production of her award-winning breakout album, *The Fame*.

Turning Point

Germanotta was able to focus on her music full-time once she did not have to attend classes or complete homework assignments. During the day, she worked at an internship for Famous Music Publishing, where she made copies of press releases and performed other administrative tasks. By night, she continued to perform in nightclubs with the SGBand. One evening in January 2006, her band was playing in the same club as singer and talent scout Wendy Starland. She and Starland had met once before, when Starland visited the Famous Music Publishing offices to speak with Germanotta's boss. Germanotta confessed to being a fan at their first meeting and told Starland she had been listening to one of her songs repeatedly. At the time, Germanotta did not

Singer/songwriter/talent scout Wendy Starland arranged an audition with producer Rob Fusari for Stefani Germanotta.

leave a lasting impression on Starland, who viewed her as conservative and mousy. In fact, when Germanotta approached her the night they were to play in the same club, Starland had low expectations for her performance.

The night the SGBand shared a stage with Starland turned out to be a turning point in Germanotta's career. Starland remembers thinking that the SGBand was terrible, but once she heard Germanotta sing, she was floored by her raw talent. Germanotta did not know it, but Starland had been tasked by producer Rob Fusari to find a strong female vocalist for an upcoming project. Germanotta's voice, energy, and piano skills had Starland on the phone to Fusari that very night. She called the producer to tell him she had found his next "it" girl.

How Lady Gaga Got Her Name

When Fusari met Germanotta, he doubted she would turn out to be the powerhouse rock vocalist he was searching for. Fusari says of their first meeting, "I'm thinking to myself, 'Please tell me this is not her,' because this is not the Strokes [critically acclaimed New York City rock band] girl I'd envisioned." Still, he gave her a chance to audition. Fusari immediately recognized that Germanotta was special when she played a song she wrote on the piano. "In 20 seconds," Fusari said, "I knew this girl would change my life."[14] They decided to work together, and Germanotta took the bus from New York City to Fusari's studio in Livingston, New Jersey, every day for a year. They formed a close bond, became romantically involved, and exchanged frequent text messages whenever they were apart.

Though there are several stories about how Germanotta got the name Lady Gaga, the most widely accepted version is that Fusari likened her vocal style to that of Freddie Mercury, the deceased lead singer for 1970s British rock band Queen. Whenever Germanotta entered his studio, Fusari greeted her by blasting the Queen song, "Radio Ga Ga." In one of Fusari's text messages to Germanotta in which he meant to reference the song "Radio Ga Ga," he accidentally typed "Lady Gaga." Germanotta was brainstorming ideas for a stage name at the time, and when she received the "Lady Gaga" text message, she replied with, "That's it! Don't ever call me Stefani again."[15]

Def Jam Letdown

After she chose her stage name, Lady Gaga was more driven than ever to define her musical style and write a hit song. Most of the songs she and Fusari wrote were hard-rock or grunge, which sounded all wrong to Fusari. Though he originally sought a female lead rock vocalist, the style did not adequately showcase Gaga's talent. He proposed they switch gears and try to write pop songs with a dance beat. Gaga agreed, and in one day they wrote the song "Beautiful, Dirty, Rich," which was later included on her album *The Fame*.

Fusari knew they had a hit with "Beautiful, Dirty, Rich." He sent the recording to record executive Joshua Sarubin at Island Def Jam. Sarubin immediately set up a meeting between Gaga, Fusari, and Def Jam chair Antonio "L.A." Reid. Gaga nailed the audition, and Reid noted that she would likely transform pop music for women with her outlandish style and powerful vocals. Yet, for reasons unknown, the partnership between Gaga and

The Portal in the Park

The Portal in the Park is a children's book by (Maura) Cricket Casey published in 2006. The book contains a CD featuring Grandmaster Melle Mel rapping the book's narration, and a then-unknown Lady Gaga sings on two tracks: "World Family Tree" and "The Fountain of Truth." Casey asked Stefani Germanotta to participate in the project after seeing the pre-Gaga Germanotta perform at New York's Bitter End. The original printing of the book has only a minor mention of Lady Gaga, but subsequent printings feature her prominently.

Def Jam lasted just three months before she was dropped from the label. Gaga was devastated by the rejection and briefly considered giving up on becoming a star. Fusari encouraged Gaga to take a short break and spend time with her family while he considered their next move.

Shortly after the Def Jam letdown, Fusari introduced Lady Gaga to producer RedOne, who would eventually cowrite her popular hits "Just Dance," "Boys Boys Boys," and "Poker Face." She said of meeting the producer, "RedOne is like the heart and soul of my universe. I met him and he completely, one hundred and fifty thousand percent wrapped his arms around my talent, and it was like we needed to work together."[16] The successful collaboration between Gaga and RedOne energized Fusari to secure another recording contract. He contacted his friend Vincent Herbert from Streamline Records, a division of Interscope Records. Herbert recognized Lady Gaga's star power and signed the budding superstar to her second major record label—all by the time she was nineteen years old.

Gaga Dances Burlesque

Lady Gaga was reinvigorated by her partnership with RedOne and her new recording deal with Streamline/Interscope. She started to dress more outlandishly and behaved as if she was already a superstar. She told everyone to stop calling her Stefani (including close friends and family) and often referred to herself in the third person as simply "Lady Gaga." She and Fusari drifted apart and eventually stopped dating. Gaga worked on her songs with RedOne and started performing in neo-burlesque shows throughout the Lower East Side's underground club scene.

Lady Gaga was drawn to neo-burlesque because of its new ("neo") take on burlesque (theatrical performances that often include striptease, comedy, and attention-getting gimmicks, such as fire breathing and acrobatics). Neo-burlesque blends the go-go dancer and cabaret performance styles and was a perfect fit for Gaga's talent and theatrical stage presence. She sang her songs wearing skimpy yet elaborate costumes and performed sexy dance routines that included elements of physical comedy

Lady Gaga worked on her songs with producer RedOne and started performing neo-burlesque shows in Manhattan's Lower East Side nightclubs.

and striptease. It was an ideal job, because she was able to express her artistic side, hone her entertainment style, and earn enough money to pay the bills.

Gaga was exploding with creative energy, and she worked day and night on her act. She experimented with cocaine and often stayed up all night to write songs. Lady Gaga was in creative overdrive, and she rarely took breaks or rested. Brendan Sullivan, Gaga's disc jockey at the time, remembers Gaga sewing costumes by hand for her go-go performances while they discussed her future aspirations. Sullivan noticed even then that people stared at her in public, as if she was already a celebrity. He mused that she behaved as though she was already famous: "She didn't dream of fame. She announced it."[17] One afternoon, she wrote in one of his notebooks, "There is a musical government who decides what we all get to hear and listen to. And I want to be one of those people."[18]

Disappointing Daddy

Lady Gaga was more focused than she had ever been, and she could sense that fame and success were just around the corner. But her "fame-at-any-cost" attitude came at a price: the loss of her beloved father's respect. Joseph Germanotta did not agree with his daughter's decision to leave Tisch, but he understood her need to take a break from college and explore her craft in the real world. He always loved and supported his daughter, and so it was no surprise when he went to see one of Gaga's performances. Nothing could have prepared Joseph for the shock he felt during his daughter's show. She danced burlesque, wearing only a leopard-print G-string and tank top. She appeared to be high on drugs, and Joseph feared that his classically trained daughter had gone insane. Lady Gaga said of that night, "He thought I was nuts—that I was doing drugs and had lost my mind. . . . For my father, it was an issue of sanity."[19]

Joseph argued with Gaga after the show and told her she was wasting her talent. He urged her to recognize that she was spending time with people who were using her and would ruin her chances of success. He was so disappointed that he did not see or speak to his daughter for several months. Joseph's absence was a wake-up call for Gaga. She could not stand that she had let her father down, so she stopped doing drugs and worked to regain her father's respect. Though she agreed with her father that her drug use would ruin her life—and her career—she did not give up performing burlesque. She continued to dance in bars throughout New York City, which led her to meet and fall in love with bar manager Luc Carl.

Lady Gaga and the Starlight Revue

Lady Gaga fell hard and fast for Carl soon after they began dating. He epitomized everything she wanted in a boyfriend: He looked and behaved like a rock star. Through him, she met Lady Starlight, a hard-rock disc jockey and go-go dancer at St. Jerome's, the bar Carl managed. The ladies made an immediate connection at Gaga's twentieth birthday party, where they decided to combine their shows into one act called *Lady Gaga and the Starlight Revue*. They performed Gaga's songs, with Gaga on the piano and Starlight as beat master and disc jockey. Their shows were known as "The Ultimate Pop Burlesque Rockshow," and they became a cult favorite of the Lower East Side underground club scene. Fans loved the ladies' retro-1970s-style show, which always included wild rock-star antics. They stripped down to their underwear, lit hairspray cans on fire, and belted out early versions of songs that would later become tracks on *The Fame*.

Gaga and Starlight's tribute to 1970s-era variety acts gained popularity and eventually won them a spot at the Lollapalooza music festival in Chicago's Grant Park in 2007. Other acts at the festival that year included Pearl Jam, Modest Mouse, Amy Winehouse, and the Yeah Yeah Yeahs. The ladies recognized this as a great opportunity, and they jumped at the chance to perform for such a large audience.

Then unknown to the majority of the Lollapalooza audience, Gaga made a splash when she appeared onstage in black underwear, a thin silver belt, fishnet stockings, and a homemade disco-ball bikini top. However, many people in the crowd confused the dark-haired Gaga with Amy Winehouse, who was scheduled to perform the next night. Producer Vincent Herbert, who had used his own money to send Gaga to Lollapalooza, was concerned that Gaga would forever be confused with Winehouse if she did not immediately change her look. He told her to dye her dark hair blonde to save her career, which she did without question.

Lady Gaga performs with the Starlight Revue at Lollapalooza in 2007.

The Industry Pays Attention

After her well-received Lollapalooza performance, Lady Gaga learned that the record industry was a tight-knit community where everybody knew each other. This could either work for or against an artist, but in Gaga's case, it was beneficial to her career. She was able to parlay her administrative internship

Lady Gaga and New Kids on the Block

Lady Gaga was the opening act for New Kids on the Block (NKOTB) during their 2008 reunion tour. She had been signed to Interscope Records, and NKOTB were label mates. Gaga was commissioned to write material for their album *The Block*. She wrote and appeared as a featured guest on the track "Big Girl Now" and also toured with NKOTB from October to November 2008 to promote her first major release, *The Fame*.

Lady Gaga performs her opening act for her tour with New Kids on the Block.

with Famous Music Publishing into a gig writing songs for established artists at Interscope. This was a key career move that expanded her reputation among record executives.

In the spring of 2007, Sony/ATV Music Publishing signed a publishing deal with Lady Gaga. This contracted her to write songs for performers such as Britney Spears ("Quicksand"), New Kids on the Block ("Big Girl Now"), and the Pussycat Dolls ("Elevator"). Jody Gerson, who signed the publishing deal between Lady Gaga and Sony/ATV, immediately recognized Gaga's star power. She said of meeting her, "She blew me away from the moment I met her."[20] At last, Lady Gaga felt like industry insiders were beginning to notice her.

Realizing *The Fame*

Lady Gaga worked tirelessly to make the right connections. She continued to write songs for other artists, work on her own music, and collaborate with any artist who would have her. Once again, Lady Gaga's determination paid off when she caught the attention of rhythm-and-blues performer/producer Akon. Gaga sang guide vocals for one of his songs (guide vocals, or reference vocals, act as a place holder for lyrics yet-to-be-recorded to show how the pitch and melody should sound), and Akon immediately appreciated Lady Gaga's powerful voice. His instincts told him that she was far too talented to remain a reference vocalist, and he wanted to help her become a star. He quickly obtained permission from Interscope chair Jimmy Iovine to sign Gaga to his label, Kon Live Distribution. Akon was an early believer that Gaga was destined to be a megastar, and he said of meeting her, "She was definitely a blessing. She came at the right moment. I'm glad I believed in her, boy."[21]

Once Gaga was under Akon's umbrella, she had access to all of the people and recording equipment necessary to record her first album, *The Fame*. Lady Gaga chose the title to reflect the theme of the album, which she described in the following way: "The music is intended to inspire people to feel a certain way about themselves, so they'll be able to encompass, in their own lives, a sense of inner fame that they can project to the world."[22]

Rhythm and blues performer/producer Akon signed Lady Gaga because he believed she had a powerful voice and was destined for superstardom.

Gaga reconnected with RedOne, and together with Rob Fusari, Akon, and producer Martin Kierszenbaum, they wrote nearly all of the songs for the album in just one week. *The Fame* included a staggering number of soon-to-be smash hits, such as "Just Dance," "Poker Face," "Paparazzi," "Beautiful, Dirty, Rich," and "LoveGame." Gaga composed the songs on the piano first, and then sang the vocals for all of the tracks in one take. She then went back and spent just a few hours recording the harmonies for each song. Everyone who worked with her on the album was amazed by how effortlessly the music flowed from her.

Lady Gaga, however, was not surprised by the speed with which *The Fame* came together. After all, she had worked on early versions of many of the album's songs for years before they were recorded. Gaga always knew she would write a hit record and has said of the experience, "A hit record writes itself. Once you tap into the soul, the song begins to write itself."[23]

Gaga Gets Famous

Interscope released *The Fame* on August 19, 2008, to mostly critical acclaim. Dance music fans around the world devoured the first single, "Just Dance," which was released months before the full-length album. The song became a dance anthem in

Rob Fusari's Lawsuit Against Lady Gaga

In March 2010, producer Rob Fusari filed a $30 million lawsuit against two of Lady Gaga's companies. In the suit, Fusari claimed that he created the Lady Gaga name, encouraged her to drop rock music for dance beats, and cowrote Gaga's hit "Paparazzi" as well as two other songs. Fusari said the $30 million figure derived from a 2006 contract between him and Gaga's Team Love Child (a corporate entity he claimed he cocreated with Gaga to promote her career) and Mermaid Music. Gaga's attorney maintained that Fusari's deal with Gaga was unlawful and filed a countersuit. Fusari dropped the lawsuit in September 2010, and it was unclear whether there was an out-of-court settlement.

nightclubs around the globe, but especially in gay dance clubs. Gaga was fast becoming a pop-disco diva, and her fans were eager to hear the rest of her grooves.

Most of the album's initial success occurred abroad in the United Kingdom, Australia, Ireland, and Canada. It took longer for the record to catch on in the United States. American critics gave the album mixed reviews, but Gaga was undeterred. Instead, she launched an exhaustive campaign to promote the album. Gaga's promotional assault included television performances on *So You Think You Can Dance*, *Jimmy Kimmel Live!*, *The Tonight Show with Jay Leno*, *The Hills*, and the *Miss Universe* beauty pageant. She also performed as the opening act for New Kids on the Block during the North American leg of their *Live!* tour in the fall of 2008.

Lady Gaga was finally in a position to reveal her superstardom to the world. She was determined to top the charts worldwide and show her critics that she was no flash-in-the-pan pop star. The savvy entertainer knew she must not rest or become comfortable with her success. Rather, she used her early success as motivation to work harder to prove to the world that Lady Gaga was here to stay.

The Year of Gaga

Lady Gaga relentlessly promoted *The Fame* throughout the fall of 2008 and into 2009—a decision that paid off in record sales, positive reviews, and an exponential increase in her fan base. She continued to book performance slots on television shows both within the United States and abroad, which allowed her to reach millions of new fans worldwide. Her opening act for New Kids on the Block was well received by audiences, and with each live performance, Gaga's record sales increased, as did her critical acclaim.

In 2009, the overwhelmingly positive response from critics and fans to *The Fame* eventually catapulted Gaga's music to the top of the charts in the United States. By the end of the year, she had five top-ten songs on *Billboard* magazine's Top 100 list. However, she did not coast on her newfound success. On the contrary, she viewed her achievement as a sign to work harder to satisfy her growing legion of Gaga-crazed fans. Thus, she began her first solo world tour and released her second album while the first was still dominating the airwaves.

The Fame Ball Tour

On March 12, 2009, Lady Gaga kicked off her first solo world tour at the House of Blues in San Diego, California. In less than thirty days, she headlined more than nineteen concerts. Each show sold out quickly, and in many cases additional seats and

Lady Gaga kicked off her first solo world tour at the House of Blues in San Diego, California, on March 12, 2009.

shows had to be added to accommodate the throngs of fans who wanted to see Lady Gaga live. *The Fame Ball* tour lasted just six months, but Gaga performed more than seventy shows throughout North America, Asia, and Europe. She frequently says that touring is important to her because she feeds off the energy of her live audiences. Indeed, Gaga seems to thrive on a rigorous tour schedule that would overwhelm other performers.

The tour received mostly positive reviews from critics, even from those who had previously doubted Gaga's pop music significance. Said Jill Menze of *Billboard*, "Lady Gaga has proven herself to be an of-the-moment pop sensation. Dig deeper, and it's clear she's versatile and talented enough to have staying power."[24] Not all reviews were glowing, however. Whitney Pastorek of *Entertainment Weekly* criticized Gaga when she referred to her banter with the audience as silly.

The Monster Ball Tour

Negative reviews of her performances were rare, though. Gaga's commitment to theatrics, her powerful vocals, and her competency on the piano—as well as her sheer creativity—forced even critics to admit that she was a tour de force. Gaga, however, was less concerned with pleasing critics and more interested in cultivating a relationship with her fans.

To this end, Gaga launched *The Monster Ball* tour, which kicked off on November 27, 2009, in Montreal, Canada. Shows immediately sold out everywhere Gaga was to perform, which included cities in North America, Europe, Asia, and Oceania. As with *The Fame Ball* tour, most cities added extra dates, booked larger venues, and added more seats to accommodate Gaga's

Transmission Gagavision

Lady Gaga is extraordinarily media and Internet savvy. In June 2008, months before her debut album was released, Gaga began a weekly Web series about her quest to become a cultural phenomenon. Called *Transmission Gagavision*, the series comprised forty episodes and ran through March 2009. Each broadcast began with the tagline "Lady Gaga has been sent to Earth to infiltrate human culture one sequin at a time," spoken in a synthesized voice. The episodes took the form of a behind-the-scenes look at the life of Lady Gaga and served as an invitation to fans or potential fans to take part in her ascent to global stardom.

The Haus of Gaga, *Transmission Gagavision*, episode 1. www.thehausofgaga.com/videos/transmission-gagavision.

ever-expanding fan base. And ever-expanding it was: when Gaga kicked off her first tour at the House of Blues in San Diego, she played for about 1,000 people. When she went back to play the San Diego Sports Arena just nine months later, the seating capacity had to be increased from 6,000 to 10,800 seats. Later shows in larger venues that held more than 35,000 people sold out almost immediately after tickets went on sale.

The response by fans was so positive that Gaga scheduled tour dates through April 2011. She admits that she thrives on the energy of her fans and that she requires their applause to keep motivated. During one performance in 2010, Gaga told the crowd, "I'm like Tinker Bell. You know how, with Tinker Bell, if you don't applaud her, her light goes out? Speak for me! Do you want me to die?"[25] The answer from fans, critics, and the music industry was a resounding no. They want as much of Gaga as she is willing to give, and she is always more than happy to grant their wish.

Lady Gaga performs in front of a packed house in Japan on The Monster Ball *tour. Shows sold out everywhere she played.*

An Elaborate and Outlandish Performer

Lady Gaga quickly became known as an elaborate and outlandish performer who pushes the envelope of modern musical entertainment. She earned this reputation in 2009 with a succession of increasingly outrageous performances.

She first sent shock waves through the American entertainment industry when she appeared in an elimination episode of *American Idol* in April 2009. The eccentric singer performed her hit single "Poker Face" beneath pink stage lights and played a clear piano filled with bubbles. Once the song hit its groove, she danced her routine while wearing a space-age, pants-less outfit complete with a zipper eye patch. In his review of the performance, MTV News correspondent Gil Kaufman summed up the sentiments of many spectators when he said, "*American Idol* has never seen anything like Lady Gaga" and predicted that "*Idol* may never be the same again."[26] The performance was so popular that show creator and prickly judge Simon Cowell later asked Lady Gaga to become a mentor for *Idol* performers. Though she declined the offer, Gaga recognized the significance of Cowell's invitation.

Gaga's appearance on *American Idol* made her one of the most sought-after guest entertainers on hit television shows throughout 2009. With each appearance, her performances became more theatrical, her costumes more outrageous, and her sets more elaborate.

Her trademark outlandish theatrics were also on full display at the 2009 *MTV Video Music Awards* (VMAs), where Lady Gaga was nominated for several Moonmen Awards and also performed during the show. The millions of viewers who tuned in to the VMAs were treated to one of Gaga's most talked-about performances. Her dazzling rendition of her hit single "Paparazzi" was framed by an elaborate Gothic background with an ornately decorated, giant staircase. Her set opened with the crashing sound of an enormous, fallen crystal chandelier, with Gaga lying in its wreckage. Backup dancers dressed in white twirled around her and raised her up as she belted out her number.

Lady Gaga sent shock waves through the American entertainment business when she performed her hit "Paparazzi" on the 2009 MTV Video Music Awards.

She wowed the star-studded audience when she banged furiously on her white piano, with one leg propped up on the keys. The truly shocking moment came, however, toward the end of the song when fake blood suddenly poured down Gaga's body and she was hung by her arm above the stage. The camera zoomed in on Gaga's face, which was motionless. Fake blood oozed from one of her eyes, and Gaga's "lifeless" body dangled high above the stage as the thunderous noise of cameras taking photos blared through the sound system. Gaga's statement about fame and its consequences washed over the awestruck, yet thoroughly entertained audience. A triumphant Lady Gaga went on to win three VMAs: Best Art Direction and Best Special Effects for her "Paparazzi" video, and Best New Artist.

The Fame Monster Is Released

Lady Gaga is a self-described workaholic, and so it was no surprise that her increased notoriety energized her to release her second album, *The Fame Monster*, in November 2009. Gaga aggressively promoted *The Fame Monster* even before its release. She performed the first few singles from the album on *Saturday Night Live* in October 2009 and also at the Los Angeles Museum of Contemporary Art's 30th Anniversary Celebration. In the weeks leading up to the album's official release, Gaga's first single from the album, "Bad Romance," had fans and critics buzzing about what the rest of the album might sound like.

The album was well received, and the music review website Pitchfork ranked "Bad Romance" at number thirty-nine in their Top 100 singles from 2009. Reviewer David Drake lauded Gaga in his review when he said, "'Bad Romance' was the moment where the music didn't just live up to the (self-inflated) hype, but surpassed it. The track is epic in construction."[27] Gaga's appeal was catching on as fans and critics alike realized that she was an indomitable performer who had no intention of slowing down.

Lady Gaga's popularity went viral once radio stations, dance clubs, and popular television shows began to play her music regularly. Her first single, "Just Dance," went four times Platinum in December 2009 after it sold more than 4 million copies. The dance anthem spent five months on *Billboard* magazine's Hot 100 list, during which time her second single, "Poker Face," also made the hit list. Gaga became the first artist in more than a decade to have two consecutive singles on the Hot 100. "Love-Game" and "Paparazzi" also made the list while the other songs were still on it, which sealed Gaga's position as the queen of *Billboard* magazine's Hot 100. In fact, *The Fame* has the distinction of remaining in the number one slot on the *Billboard* Dance/Electronica Albums chart longer than any other album in history, a position which it held for seventy-nine weeks.

Gaga broke more records at the 2010 *MTV Video Music Awards*, where she set the record for the most nominations in the history of the VMAs, with thirteen nominations. Gaga accepted the award for the show's top honor, Video of the Year for her "Bad Romance" video, before millions of viewers. Gaga not only took the biggest award of the night, but left with seven other Moonmen. As a result, she tied the band a-ha for the 1986 record for winning the second-highest number of VMAs in one night (singer Peter Gabriel won the most VMAs in one night when he was awarded ten Moonmen in 1987).

OMGaga! on *Gossip Girl*

Cementing Lady Gaga's status as queen of pop culture, in 2009 several songs from *The Fame* and *The Fame Monster* were featured in episodes of the hit television series *Gossip Girl*, the top-rated show among teen girls. Gaga herself appeared in the episode "The Last Days of Disco Stick," which aired on November 16, 2009. *Gossip Girl* is known for being on the cutting edge of the teenage social scene, most especially in regards to fashion and

Lady Gaga accepts the Music Video of the Year Award from presenter Cher at the 2010 MTV Video Music Awards for her "Bad Romance" video.

music. Thus, Gaga's inclusion was significant because it meant the creators of the show deemed her music hot enough for its trendy viewers. Partnering with the show was a savvy move for Gaga's career. The former outcast's affiliation with *Gossip Girl* put her on the radar of millions of mainstream tweens, teens, and twentysomethings—a demographic she might not have been able to reach until much later in her career.

Soon after Gaga's appearance on *Gossip Girl*, she performed at the 2009 *American Music Awards* in Los Angeles, California. Though she was nominated for several awards, she did not win in any category, which surprised critics and disappointed fans. Still, those who tuned in were treated to an outrageous performance of her hit singles "Bad Romance" and "Speechless."

Gaga wore a flesh-colored bodysuit with white, glowing ribs as she stomped, danced, and dominated the ultramodern set.

Lady Gaga Puts Tour Ahead of Health

Lady Gaga is so devoted to her Little Monsters that she refuses to let exhaustion keep her from performing. Although she had to cancel a show in January 2010 at Purdue University after fainting an hour before she was to go on, she went on *The Oprah Winfrey Show* the following day to apologize to fans. She then had the show rescheduled. She also came close to fainting onstage during a March 2010 performance of "Bad Romance" in New Zealand but finished the song and kept the tour rolling despite its obvious toll on her.

When she transitioned from "Bad Romance" to "Speechless," Gaga used her microphone stand to smash a large glass box that encased her piano. An astonished audience watched as Gaga mounted her piano bench and banged out the opening notes to her guttural ballad. The performance intensified when Gaga's piano suddenly erupted in flames. Violinists who accompanied Gaga wore gas masks and stood in another glass enclosure. Gaga took her exhibition even further when she smashed one glass bottle after another against her piano to accentuate the drama of her performance.

In the last moments of her appearance, Lady Gaga stood up, covered in glass, with her piano still in flames behind her. The crowd roared to its feet with a standing ovation. The performance sealed Gaga's place as one of the most groundbreaking entertainers of her time.

Gaga's Little Monsters

Such riveting performances, along with her hard work, tireless self-promotion, and eventual critical accolades, led Lady Gaga's fan base to grow exponentially in 2009. One night in Boston during *The Monster Ball* tour, such fans earned an official name. Lady Gaga announced she had been nominated for five Grammy Awards, and her fans went wild. She thanked them effusively, calling them her "little monsters." The nickname stuck, and her millions of fans were thereafter referred to—by fans, Gaga, and the media—as her "Little Monsters."

Lady Gaga made permanent her adoration for her fans when she had "Little Monsters" tattooed on the arm she uses to hold the microphone. She dedicated the tattoo to her fans on Twitter soon after she had it done. Her Twitter post included a link to a picture of the tattoo with the Tweet, "look what i did last night. little monsters forever, on the arm that holds my mic. xx"[28] Gaga has said on more than one occasion that she would die without—and for—her Little Monsters.

Lady Gaga performs for her Little Monsters during an episode of the **Today** *show on July 9, 2010.*

Gaga shows her love for her fans by communicating regularly with them through her various social media outlets. Indeed, her fans are always in the know because her Facebook page and Twitter account are updated at least daily. In July 2010, she surpassed President Barack Obama when she accumulated more than 10 million Facebook fans. Then in August 2010, Gaga replaced Britney Spears as the "Queen of Twitter" when she logged more than 5.7 million followers on Twitter. In addition, there is an application for the iPhone that keeps her Little Monsters in the loop about tour information, news, and whatever else Gaga wants to say to them. This feature also allows users to view episodes of her Internet show *Transmission Gagavision*, as well as to engage in live chats with other fans and members of Gaga's applications team.

Slammed by *Slant* and Others

Lady Gaga received mostly rave reviews on her live performances, and she played for sold-out crowds throughout her tour. Yet many attacked her music, style, and videos and even claimed to hate her.

One of the most critical reviews of *The Fame* was levied by reviewer Sal Cinquemani of *Slant* magazine. Cinquemani gave the album a two-and-a-half star rating (out of five). He complained, "Gaga's lyrics alternate between cheap drivel . . . and nonsensical drivel . . . and her vocal performances are uneven at best."[29] Cinquemani's few positive comments about the album were cloaked in criticism, too. For example, he said that "Poker Face" and other songs on the album "rest almost solely on their snappy production and sing-along hooks."[30]

Washington Post staff writer J. Freedom du Lac also accused Gaga of being wholly derivative of other acts. He claimed there was nothing original about Gaga's music or style. Du Lac described the song "Paper Gangsta" as a "train wreck of borrowed ideas," and said the rest of the songs on *The Fame* "come across as flat and faceless, not to mention vapid."[31] The critic argued that Gaga was a patchwork star who had taken her name from a Queen song, her style from the Pussycat Dolls and Madonna, and her sound from Gwen Stefani, Rihanna, Pink, and Britney Spears.

Gaga has also been accused by performance artist Brooke Aldridge, known as "Lolly Pop," of copying her music and style. Lolly Pop claims that Gaga's 2010 single "Telephone" is a rip-off of her 2004 song "Life on Hold." Though music critic Chris Riemenschneider is not convinced by Lolly Pop's claim, he wrote in a 2010 *Washington Post* review, "Gaga is indeed a copycat who freely lifts her outrageous style, mostly vapid songs and club-girl personality from other performers."[32]

The *Slant* and *Washington Post* reviews were representative of the reasons Gaga's detractors criticize her. Indeed, Lady Gaga is most often denounced for being a copy of other acts, including Christina Aguilera, Gwen Stefani, Britney Spears, and Grace Jones. Jones, who is a former model, singer, and outlandish fashion icon from the 1970s and 1980s, has been very vocal about her disdain for Gaga. Jones went so far as to refuse an offer to collaborate with Gaga on an album, commenting, "I'd just prefer to work with someone who is more original and someone who is not copying me, actually."[33] Jones was not alone in her observation of Gaga as a copycat. Sri Lankan songwriter M.I.A., for example, has accused her of being nothing more than a "good mimic."[34]

Stolen Material, Girl

Lady Gaga has perhaps been most criticized for failing to pay homage to her biggest influence, Madonna. Die-hard Madonna fans delight in pointing out all of the ways in which they think Lady Gaga pilfers Madonna's music, fashion, and videos. They claim Gaga is a copycat who has capitalized on Madonna's trailblazing career. From her cone-shaped brassieres to the melodies of many of her songs, Gaga is pegged as a shameless Madonna mimic. The Facebook pages "Lady Gaga Is Just a Copy of Madonna" and "I Hate Lady Gaga" give Gaga haters a place to voice their complaints. The latter boasts more than thirty-two thousand fans, and both contain arguments for the ways in which Gaga "rips off" Madonna.

Despite intense rivalry among fans, Lady Gaga and Madonna have a cordial relationship of mutual respect.

In reality, however, there is no animosity between Lady Gaga and Madonna (in interviews, both women have had only nice things to say about each other). The two pop divas gave a humorous nod to the buzz surrounding their relationship when they shared a guest appearance on a *Saturday Night Live* skit on

October 4, 2009. Their parody consisted of having Madonna "attack" Lady Gaga onstage after the pair argues over who is hotter. They pull each other's hair in a fake fight, and Madonna wrestles Gaga to the ground. The skit ends with an interrupted makeup kiss between the pop queens. Gaga-lovers embraced the performance because it poked fun at the Madonna-Gaga comparisons with humor and lightheartedness, though the skit only gave Gaga haters more fuel for their fire.

For every Gaga hater out there, though, there are many more fans who self-identify as one of Gaga's Little Monsters. In fact, Lady Gaga's official Facebook page holds the distinction of having the most fans of any living person. Indeed, as of August 2010, Gaga has more than 14 million fans—many more than the "I Hate Lady Gaga" fan page. Gaga has created a positive-feedback loop with her fans through Facebook and Twitter, and she does not focus on her detractors. Rather, she is committed to building up her entertainment empire and creating her whole celebrity self.

Chapter 4

Designing Gaga

Everything Lady Gaga does is by design to enhance her celebrity image. Indeed, such painstaking attention is paid to Gaga's music, choreography, set design, performance art, and wardrobe that it takes a team of risk-taking artists and designers to create the iconic Lady Gaga.

Fashion Statement

Lady Gaga is perhaps most often recognized for her outrageous wardrobe. She is frequently photographed without pants while wearing gigantic heel-less hoof boots. Her costumes often feature bizarre, even unnerving, fabrics or items. For example, she raised eyebrows when she accepted the 2009 Best New Artist MTV Video Music Award dressed in a red lace ensemble that completely covered her face. She also created one of the most photographed meetings ever for the paparazzi when she greeted Queen Elizabeth wearing a red latex dress and outlandish, sparkling-red, see-through eye patches. Though many people consider Gaga's fashion sense to be over-the-top, even ridiculous, some clothing designers are inspired to create unusual outfits for her. Indeed, her style, celebrity, and willingness to take fashion risks make Lady Gaga fun to dress.

Designers who have created outfits for Lady Gaga include Alexander McQueen, Chanel, Viktor & Rolf, Jean Charles de Castelbajac, and Giorgio Armani. Gaga most often dons Armani's creations at big, high-profile events, such as at the Grammy Awards, the Metropolitan Museum of Art's Costume Institute Gala, onstage during *The Monster Ball* tour, and on *American Idol* in May 2010.

Armani particularly enjoys outfitting Gaga because of her free spirit and ability to wear (or not wear) just about anything. For example, Armani's *American Idol* costume had Gaga onstage in a black mesh bodysuit that covered her face. The barely-there suit was decorated with Chantilly lace inlayed with intricate crystal beadwork. The outfit was topped off with a black silk organza (type of fabric) cape and hood. Armani expressed his pleasure in designing the ensemble for Gaga when he said, "To complement the spirit of Lady Gaga herself, I have let my imagination run free, and the outfit I have created for her for

Lady Gaga meets Queen Elizabeth II of Great Britain in one of the most photographed incidents of her photogenic career.

American Idol is pure fantasy."[35] Their shared vision for fantasy couture has allowed Lady Gaga and Giorgio Armani to create an unforgettable fashion statement.

Alexander McQueen's Muse

It was Gaga's relationship with designer Alexander McQueen, however, that most often caught the media's attention. McQueen's controversial designs naturally made him gravitate toward the eccentric Gaga. The unconventional designer, who also worked with David Bowie, Rihanna, and Björk, created dark, even grotesque couture. Gaga was attracted to—and influenced by—some of McQueen's most famous clothing lines, with names such as Jack the Ripper, Highland Rape, and The Birds. His Gothic designs often included corsets made from animal bones and skins, feathers, lace, and extremely high-heeled shoes and boots. One of his most famous creations donned by Gaga was the see-through red lace ensemble that she wore to accept her Moonman Award at the 2009 *MTV Video Music Awards*.

Gaga has been photographed hundreds of times in such McQueen originals, and all of the outfits have incorporated some or all of his signature materials. For a while, it seemed as if Gaga wore only McQueen. This led Amber Jones of the celebrity news website PopEater to quip that Gaga was "nothing short of a walking McQueen ad."[36]

The trendy pair seemed to affirm this observation when they teamed up for Lady Gaga's "Bad Romance" video. In it, Gaga sported McQueen's bejeweled lobster-claw shoes—10-inch stiletto heels (25.4cm) with the foot rounded downward—for the first time. The shoes sent a ripple through the fashion industry when several models refused to wear them on the runway. The extremely uncomfortable, remarkably high heels caused the models to fear they would fall on the catwalk. Gaga, however, was undeterred. In fact, all of the outrageous outfits and footwear Gaga wears in the "Bad Romance" video were created by McQueen. Their connection was so strong that the designer's

Alexander McQueen's Suicide

Designer Alexander McQueen referred to Lady Gaga as his muse. Her song "Bad Romance" had its premiere at the close of his Paris fashion show, and many of his designs adorned Lady Gaga and the dancers in the song's video.

The fashion world suffered a loss when McQueen committed suicide in February 2010 shortly after his mother died. Upon receiving the news, Gaga Tweeted a silent farewell— she posted a picture on Twitter of herself embracing the designer (the post included no explanatory text). A few days later, Gaga stole the show at the BRIT Awards with a performance of shortened versions of "Telephone" and "Dance in the Dark," which she dedicated to McQueen. The stage was decorated with a huge statue of Gaga wearing McQueen's signature lobster-claw platform shoes, which she had worn in the "Bad Romance" video.

Lady Gaga wowed the press and fans when she wore an Alexander McQueen design to the 2010 MTV Video Music Awards.

publicist referred to Gaga as McQueen's "unofficial Muse."[37] Thus, Gaga was among those most devastated when the forty-year-old designer committed suicide in February 2010.

The Haus of Gaga

Though Lady Gaga is a magnet for high-profile fashion designers to test daring new clothing lines, the majority of her costumes are designed in-house. In yet another expression of her desire to be unique, Lady Gaga has assembled a creative team to help her remain on the cutting edge of the entertainment industry. This group of designers, artists, inventors, and tech geeks are collectively known as the Haus of Gaga.

Gaga was inspired to form the Haus by pop artist Andy Warhol. In the 1960s, Warhol's collaboration with other creative types was known as "the Factory." Together, members of the Factory mass-produced his famous silk-screen pop art, made movies, and joined forces on countless other artistic endeavors. Lady Gaga was motivated to start the Haus after she read Warhol's book *The Philosophy of Andy Warhol: From A to B and Back Again.*

The Haus of Gaga is responsible for all things Gaga. The collective is divided into creative teams that each work to enhance, support, and reinvent Gaga's image, style, and live performances. Gaga's goal in assembling the team was to marry all aspects of art, music, and performance to form a complete entertainment package. She explains her ambition in the following way: "It's all about everything altogether—performance art, pop performance art, fashion. . . . I want the imagery to be so strong that fans will want to eat and taste and lick every part of us."[38] The sole purpose of the Haus is to realize Gaga's wildest fantasies through couture, props, short films, videos, and elaborate set designs.

Gaga sometimes expresses an idea to the Haus with collages made up of clippings from magazines and newspapers. She also uses word association and visual aids, such as landmarks, to get the scope of her ideas across. Members of the Haus then break into teams to invent and design until they capture Gaga's vision. A few of the Haus of Gaga's most famous inventions include the bubble dress she wore on the June 11, 2009, cover of *Rolling Stone*, and iPod LCD glasses, which project images on little screens that are connected to an iPod. This invention was made famous in the video for "Poker Face." The Haus has also created light-up microphone gloves, hair-bow wigs, and the startlingly high heel-less hoof boots.

Lady Gaga's Haus of Gaga is a group of designers, artists, and inventors she hires to keep her fashions reinvented and on the edge of the entertainment business.

A Complete Experience

In addition to tech accessories and costume designs, the Haus also works tirelessly on complex set designs for Lady Gaga's live performances. Gaga's elaborate sets for *The Monster Ball* tour were designed to give each audience the same experience, regardless of the size or location of the venue. When Gaga described the stage design, she said, "Imagine you were to hollow out a TV and just break the fourth wall on a TV screen. It forces you to look at the center of the TV. It's my way of saying, 'My music is art.'"[39]

The Haus creates sets that offer layers of entertainment to give Lady Gaga's audience a complete performance art experience. They often project self-made short films onstage throughout Gaga's shows and suit her in costumes that are part of the set. One such example is an enormous gyroscope called "the Orbit," in which Gaga is surrounded by several moving rings. Theatrics created by the Haus for Lady Gaga's live shows have also included fake blood, a bustier that shoots flames, a bra with guns attached, a clear piano filled with bubbles, a piano engulfed by flames, and Gaga's own faked death-by-hanging.

Fashion Victim

Lady Gaga's outrageous sense of style occasionally leads to critical coverage in the media. In June 2010, she fell hard at London's Heathrow airport as a result of wearing huge, heel-less, platform hoof boots and what appeared to be a long train attached to her black leather chaps. The celebrity gossip website TMZ called her a "fashion victim," and the quip was repeated all over the Internet.

"Lady Gaga Falls Hard," TMZ.com, June 23, 2010. www.tmz.com/2010/06/23/lady-gaga-fall-heathrow-airport-boots.

A Journey Down Glitter Way

For *The Monster Ball* tour, Gaga said she was aiming for an "electro-pop-opera"[40] musical theater rendition of her act. To this end, the elaborate tour was broken down into four acts, just like a play. It told a story, with each act delivering a component of the overall theme. Loosely based on *The Wizard of Oz*, the plot sends Lady Gaga and her dancer friends down Glitter Way to get to a party. As one reviewer put it, "In Glitter Way we have a 21st-century Yellow Brick Road and in Gaga a big-city Dorothy leading her friends on the journey."[41] Gaga's entourage is moved along on their journey by her booming vocals and tightly choreographed dances. Each act has its own lavish set to conquer, but unlike Dorothy, who wants to get back home, Gaga's goal is to arrive at the ultimate celebration—*The Monster Ball*. The New York City–themed acts, titled City, Subway, Forest, and Monster Ball, divided Gaga's many hits among them.

The Haus of Gaga brought this elaborate storyline to life with jaw-dropping sets and high-tech gadgets and props. Each act of the show is separated by short films, written and directed by members of the Haus, that are projected on two giant video screens. The ambitious show includes more than fifteen costume changes for Gaga and requires around twenty-four semitrucks to haul all of the equipment. Set design included the construction of a multilevel stage that was four times the size of the original stage Gaga's team designed for *The Fame Ball* tour, a 40-foot (12m) mechanical sea monster, a giant keyboard inside a hollowed-out car, and a tornado of fire above a piano. The extravagant production was expected to generate more than $200 million in revenue by the conclusion of the tour in April 2011. Indeed, even with tickets priced (on average) at more than one hundred dollars apiece, people were willing to pay to experience Gaga's reality.

The Monster Ball tour is a prime example of why Haus of Gaga–orchestrated concerts are often compared to a supercharged opera or musical theater. As music critic Joe Brown said after he saw Lady Gaga live in Las Vegas, "Lady Gaga out-Cher-ed

Lady Gaga onstage during **The Monster Ball** *tour. The sets were designed by the Haus of Gaga.*

Cher, made *Cirque du Soleil* and Britney's 'Circus Tour' look like county fair carnivals, and made New Year's Eve in Las Vegas anticlimactic."[42] Music critics like Brown consistently validate that Gaga is an entertainment visionary. As such, she is credited for having elevated concertgoers' expectations for live performances to an impossibly high level.

Always On

Lady Gaga's music, style, performance, and image are all expressions of the entertainer living her life as art, and she never turns it off. She is the consummate celebrity, and as such, is dedicated to surpassing the expectations of her fans and critics. She is consistently able to accomplish this by being 100 percent Gaga, 100 percent of the time. She maintains that Lady Gaga is not a character that she becomes, but rather the embodiment of the person she always has been.

She no longer answers to "Stefani" and insists that even close friends and family call her "Gaga." She hates when people use her birth name. "If you know me, and you call me Stefani, you don't really know me at all,"[43] she says. She has made clear to fans, friends, family, and others that Stefani Germanotta no longer exists—there is only Gaga. Even seasoned journalists are amazed by how thoroughly "Gaga" she is. For example, when the superstar was interviewed for *New York* magazine in March 2010, author Vanessa Grigoriadis expected to get a behind-the-scenes peek at the pop diva. She was surprised to meet Gaga instead of Stefani Germanotta and wrote, "I never thought she was going to actually *be* Lady Gaga."[44]

Writer Lisa Robinson was also treated to the full Gaga experience when she interviewed her for the September 2010 issue of *Vanity Fair*. Robinson met Gaga at her home so the singer could change her clothes after a long day of filming the video for her hit single "Alejandro." Robinson was awestruck when the star appeared in her own living room dressed in full Gaga regalia. She wrote, "So much for comfort. The Gaga is encased in a skintight, black, gauzy turtleneck catsuit covered with rhinestones. Long blond wig. Face covered with black lace netting. With the [eight-inch high, heel-less] boots on." Robinson went on to describe how the eccentric celebrity only removed her veil after she had made her "Gaga entrance."[45]

Many of Gaga's artistic choices are not so well received, however. The pop star sparked reactions that ranged from mockery to outrage when she wore a Kermit the Frog frock during an interview for a German television show. The outfit had dozens of Kermit dolls attached to it, and she wore Kermit's head as a hat.

Many fans of Jim Henson (creator of Kermit and *The Muppet Show*) felt the fashionista had gone too far. They accused her of being disrespectful to the deceased Henson and said the outfit

Themes of Life and Death on Tour

Gaga uses images that range from sublime to truly horrible in *The Monster Ball* tour to create an overwhelming, immersive experience for concertgoers. Always drawn to dark images as well as the themes of death and rebirth, Gaga and her entourage walk through blood and fire and encounter disturbing images in the various scenes throughout their journey. For example, a short film of Gaga eating a bloody heart is projected onto the massive video screens, and she also dies and is reborn onstage.

During The Monster Ball *tour, Lady Gaga uses fire, fake blood, and film as stage props to create a theme of death and rebirth.*

was worn in poor taste. Other critics simply said she looked ridiculous and regarded her as a superficial clown. Gaga rebuffed critics and claimed the outfit was a tribute to Henson. In fact, she cited this incident as evidence that she lives her life as art. As she put it, "I dress this way because my whole life is art, and my whole life is performance."[46] Whether Gaga's fashion sense is ultimately a triumph or a faux pas, it is clear that her outrageous sense of style and unending dedication to art have both contributed to making Lady Gaga a household name.

Chapter 5

Media Domination, Cultural Sensation

L ady Gaga launched an all-out publicity assault when she released her first album, *The Fame*, in 2008. Her intentional
media blitz has had a massive impact on all aspects of pop culture. In November 2009, Gaga became the first artist to have
four number one hits from a debut album. In 2010, she was
listed as the most influential artist in *Time* magazine's Top 100.
She also came in at number one in *Fast Company* magazine's
2010 listing of the "Most Creative People in Business." She is
the master of self-promotion, and she uses her media savvy to
saturate pop culture with all things Gaga.

Manipulating the Media

Gaga's publicity machine is rooted in self-promotion. Gaga
promotes herself via social media outlets, public appearances,
and frequent interviews for television shows, blogs, fanzines,
newspapers, and magazines. Gaga uses these platforms to de-
liver juicy gossip and controversial tidbits about herself to
journalists. Not all of these tidbits are true, but all are cal-
culated to earn Lady Gaga airtime, press space, and nonstop
publicity.

For example, in her 2010 interview with *Vanity Fair*, Gaga
confessed to interviewer Lisa Robinson that she occasionally
uses cocaine. This admission predictably provoked outrage
and caused Gaga's name to be bandied about in the media

for weeks. Journalists, fans, and celebrities publicly debated the truth of Gaga's statement. Pop icon and recovering drug addict Boy George decried Gaga's purported drug use in his blog. He accused her of lying about the regularity of her cocaine use and even suggested she was likely hiding a serious drug addiction.

Medical experts and parents weighed in on Gaga's seemingly offhand statement as well. They condemned her casual drug use and said she promoted a glamorous image of dangerous behavior to her young fans. *Family Circle* magazine and its readers called on Gaga to behave more responsibly with her role model status. Other critics argued that Gaga lied about using cocaine altogether and that her admission to Robinson was just another publicity stunt.

Gaga talks to reporters at an event. She is media savvy and uses the media to project the image she wants.

Medical Drama

Another example of Gaga-generated drama occurred when the overworked performer passed out backstage before one of her concerts. The media speculated that Gaga was exhausted, that she was sick, that she had an eating disorder, or that she was dehydrated. The superstar denied all of the rumors and responded with vague hints that there might be a more serious medical issue. Gaga admitted she had been having heart palpitations and that she sometimes had trouble breathing. She had to cancel two of her concerts in 2010 and was treated by emergency medical personnel in Tokyo, Japan, when she struggled to catch her breath.

Fans react to Lady Gaga's cancellation of her Purdue University concert due to illness. She admitted to heart palpitations and difficulty breathing and told reporters she might have lupus.

Gaga told various news outlets that she was in the midst of a series of tests and that she might have lupus (a serious auto-immune disease). She confided to a reporter from the *London Times* that she did not want to reveal the results of the medical tests, because she did not want her fans to worry. Of course, Gaga's fans immediately flooded the web with their concerns and well wishes. Eventually, Gaga confessed to Larry King on his show, *Larry King Live,* that she had an aunt who died of lupus. She said that she had been concerned she might have the disease, but that the tests revealed that she did not. Gaga went on to tell King that she was still at risk for eventually developing lupus.

Gaga's interview with Larry King was reported on by dozens of other media outlets, including MTV News, ABC News, *USA Today*, CBS News, NBC News, and the *Huffington Post*. Quotes from Gaga about her brush with lupus were regurgitated in countless publications, which in turn spawned several articles written about the disease and who is at risk for developing it. Fans and celebrity reporters speculated on the web that perhaps Gaga did actually have the debilitating condition but was shielding her fans from the news to protect them.

No Such Thing as Bad Publicity

Regardless of whether Gaga actually has lupus or does cocaine, the publicity mileage she gained from these incidents was priceless. Like any successful public relations firm, Lady Gaga and her team operate as if there is no such thing as bad publicity. She also seems impervious to criticism and is able to spin any gaffe, snafu, or embarrassment to her advantage. As arts and entertainment writer Sam Machkovech has put it, "Pop hasn't seen such a tactically proficient media manipulator in too long."[47] In fact, Gaga turns every encounter with the public into an opportunity to promote some aspect of her entertainment package.

Gaga's biggest publicity stunts are often the most criticized. For example, she surprised fans when she jumped onstage

Gaga was heavily criticized for her antics onstage when she appeared at the Lollapalooza 2010 festival with the band Semi Precious Weapons.

during the set for her opening band, Semi Precious Weapons, at the Lollapalooza music festival in August 2010. Dressed only in a fishnet body stocking, Gaga banged on the drum kit, and then dove into the crowd. She was groped, licked, kissed, and fondled by fans as she rolled across the top of the crowd. Gaga took the stunt a step further when she started to kiss the lead singer of Semi Precious Weapons while they rolled over their fans. The incident was documented by dozens of people. Videos and photos of Gaga crowd surfing nearly nude went viral, and the entertainment news outlets reported on it for weeks after the concert.

Once again, parents of Gaga's young fans decried the pop star for setting a bad example. They accused her of putting the crowd at risk for injury or riots and expressed disgust with her skimpy outfit and sexually explicit behavior. This was no surprise to Gaga, as she often sparks outrage and disgust from parents. Indeed, some parents, religious leaders, and conservative news outlets have pegged Gaga as an immoral and dangerous figure. They regard her admitted drug use, promiscuous lyrics and style of dress, and outrageous public behavior as an attempt to corrupt America's youth. Gaga, however, seems motivated simply to provoke any response—positive *or* negative—from the media, her fans, and even others in the entertainment industry.

Show and Tell

It is impossible to ignore Lady Gaga, because of her in-your-face attitude. She works hard to keep her image in magazines, her music on the Internet and radio, and her antics in the news. She rarely escapes an outing without being photographed by the paparazzi and does not seem to care if they catch her in an embarrassing situation. She also expertly uses the Internet via Twitter, Facebook, and YouTube to keep fans, critics, and the media abuzz. As a result, images, stories, videos, Tweets, and Facebook status updates are constantly refreshed with new Gaga material.

One of the ways that Gaga uses the Internet is to generate great anticipation for her often controversial videos. She leaks information about the theme or content online but refuses to discuss details. Instead, she metes out bits of information to create a buzz of speculation. For example, the promotional buildup to the video for her hit song "Alejandro" went on for months. Gaga and the Haus filmed previews and aired them on the Internet as

Gaga Dresses like Barbara Walters and Larry King

In yet another example of Gaga's outrageous fashion sense, the singer dressed like two iconic media personalities when she was interviewed by them. She first dressed like Barbara Walters and even wore a wig that mirrored Walters's hair. Gaga did something similar in her interview with Larry King, though to a greater degree. In side-by-side photographs, Gaga appears to be an inverse Larry King, wearing sunglasses and a white shirt with a black tie and black suspenders, while King wears eyeglasses and a black shirt with a white tie and white suspenders.

teasers. Long before the video was officially released, celebrity gossips such as Perez Hilton heightened fans' anticipation with speculation about the video. They wondered what Gaga would wear, who the director would be, and whether it would live up to Gaga's earlier masterpieces.

Gaga added to the "Alejandro" frenzy when she was interviewed for a live radio talk show in Australia. She steered the conversation toward her upcoming video and announced that they would soon begin filming. However, she refused to discuss any specifics. When she was asked about the content of the video, Gaga exclaimed, "Are you absolutely mad? I would never, ever tell you! I would be more likely to lie through my teeth to you what the video's about so that you could all be surprised."[48] Of course, the hosts tried to pry the information out of her, but Gaga changed the subject.

Her masterful media manipulation surrounding the "Alejandro" video release created a sensation when the video finally aired on her website on June 8, 2010. Within the first few weeks of the video's release, it broke the record for the most-viewed video when it was watched more than 25 million times on YouTube. Since its debut, the video has been viewed more than 65 million times and has sparked numerous debates in the media about its sexualized religious content as well as its homoerotic and fascist imagery.

Bad Gaga, Good Publicity

Gaga was heavily criticized for the "Alejandro" video. The content was even considered offensive to some celebrities. Pop peer Katy Perry Tweeted about the video and condemned it as blasphemous. She went on to discuss Lady Gaga and the video in a 2010 interview with *Rolling Stone* magazine, which

Pop peer Katy Perry criticized Lady Gaga's "Alejandro" video by saying that when she puts "sex and spirituality together and shakes it up, bad things happen."

Gaga's Wild Magazine Covers

Always looking to use visual media as a means to challenge, provoke, and entertain, Lady Gaga has done some stunning magazine covers. Her first cover for *Rolling Stone* in 2009 saw her donning a bubble dress, and in 2010 she took a more aggressive and controversial approach, sporting a machine-gun brassiere. Ditching couture altogether, she appeared nude on the cover of the September 2010 *Vanity Fair*, with only a long blond wig covering her body. Although she was only partially nude on the cover of *Q* magazine's April 2010 issue, the provocative cover was banned by certain U.S. retail chains. She even dressed as a man and called herself "Jo Calderone" for her cover shoot in Japan's *Vogue Homme* (*Vogue* magazine for men).

gave Gaga more free press. Perry said, "I am sensitive . . . to Lady Gaga putting a rosary in her mouth. I think when you put sex and spirituality in the same bottle and shake it up, bad things happen."[49]

Another vocal Gaga detractor is Fox News commentator Bill O'Reilly. The conservative pundit discusses and disparages Lady Gaga so often on his show that he has been accused of being obsessed with the controversial pop diva. After the release of the extended version of the video for "Telephone," O'Reilly and his guests criticized her for inundating kids with vulgar images. The panel denounced the video, which also stars Beyoncé Knowles, for being inappropriate for young audiences. They complained Gaga was promoting homosexuality, promiscuity, and murder. Still, Gaga got what she seems to seek most often: airtime. During the heated segment, O'Reilly infuriated one of his guests when he showed a clip from the video. Indeed, the conservative group had effectively promoted Gaga's video, even though their goal was to steer people away from it. This is but one example of how Gaga's critics unwittingly contribute to her quest for media attention.

Jerry Seinfeld Versus Lady Gaga

After a bizarre display at two baseball games in New York City, Lady Gaga found herself in a media war with comedian Jerry Seinfeld. At the June 10, 2010, New York Mets vs. San Diego Padres game at Citi Field in Queens, New York, she stripped down to a rhinestone bikini and raised both of her middle fingers in defiance to fans and photographers while she was in the audience. Gaga claimed she was out to have a good time with friends and felt ambushed by the paparazzi, but her behavior outraged the comedian (and others). Officials at the ballpark moved Gaga and her friends to Seinfeld's private luxury box, which further angered him.

Gaga also caused a stir eight days later when she showed up at a Yankees vs. Mets game dressed only in an open Yankees jersey with her black bra and underwear exposed. She had been drinking beer and whiskey during the game and was obviously intoxicated when she talked her way past security to talk to the Yankees. The media had been denied immediate access to players due to Gaga's presence, and this enraged journalists, the Yankee's manager, sports fans, and, once again, Jerry Seinfeld. The comedian complained to WFAN's sports radio talk-show host Steve Somers, "This woman's a jerk. I hate her. I can't believe they put her in my box that I paid for! You give people the finger and you get upgraded? Is that the world we're living in now?"[50]

The two baseball game incidents and Jerry Seinfeld's reaction to them resulted in a swarm of media coverage dubbed "Jerry Seinfeld Versus Lady Gaga." *The Joy Behar Show*, CNN, ABC News, and *The View* all did segments during which celebrity panels were assembled to discuss the so-called war between Seinfeld and Gaga. Local and national sports programs covered Gaga's outrageous behavior, and Seinfeld's rant on WFAN was reprinted, replayed, and recycled for weeks after the incidents.

Gaga briefly addressed the incident, claiming that she had been set up and that photographers had been planted at the Mets game to hound her and make her angry. She also admitted that she drank too much alcohol at that game and that she simply wanted to celebrate a friend's birthday. Gaga the media manipulator, however, also stated that she is always aware that she will end up in the newspaper whenever she goes out in public. This statement, as well her outrageous antics in public settings, indicates that Lady Gaga is the one who sets up the press, rather than the other way around. In addition, Gaga's blasé response to the "war" with Seinfeld clearly illustrated that she did not take these incidents seriously. Nor did she demonstrate the least bit of concern when she was publicly insulted by Jerry Seinfeld on WFAN. Rather, Gaga seemed willing to let this entire episode run its course, as if she could not be bothered with it and had already moved on to her next publicity stunt.

Savvy Partnerships and Collaborations

Another way Gaga ensures a steady stream of publicity is through her collaborations with other artists, such as Beyoncé, RedOne, Akon, and Cyndi Lauper. She invests a lot of time and money in them and attributes her success, in part, to the relationships she has cultivated. Gaga often collaborates with other artists and works closely with directors, dancers, and designers on the production of her videos. The release of each highly stylized concept video is controlled by her team and is meticulously promoted over time. The orchestration of such events requires Gaga to depend on a close network of trusted friends and colleagues. Together, they control how and when her videos are released, which means that she can count on a record-breaking number of viewers.

Gaga has also struck up partnerships with companies such as Verizon, MAC Cosmetics, Polaroid, and Coca-Cola. Verizon and Coca-Cola products have appeared in her videos, Polaroid brought Gaga on as its creative director, and MAC enlisted her as the face of their Viva Glam campaign. As a result, there are Gaga ring tones for cell phones and applications for the iPhone. Several of her songs have also appeared in popular television shows like *Gossip Girl*, *The Hills*, and *Glee*. Gaga also teamed up with the fragrance company Coty to develop her own line of perfumes. All of this cross-marketing benefits Gaga's record sales and also boosts the notoriety of those with whom she collaborates.

Her system of collaboration and cross-marketing worked well when she released the videos for "Poker Face," "Telephone," and "Bad Romance." Each video led to countless covers, parodies, and copycats. "Poker Face" was covered by such unlikely artists as Daughtry and Faith No More, and it was also spoofed by Eric Cartman on the animated series *South Park*. Soldiers in Afghanistan made a video tribute to "Telephone" in which they acted, lip-synched, danced, and dressed up in homemade Gaga-esque costumes. The video was overwhelmingly popular and logged more than 5 million viewers on YouTube.

Gaga on *Glee*

The most-watched video in the history of YouTube, however, was "Bad Romance." It, too, spawned a number of tributes and parodies, but the biggest homage to the song occurred during an episode of the critically acclaimed television show *Glee*. Dubbed the "Gaga Episode" by both the cast and fans, the cast performed a knockout rendition of "Bad Romance," which was hailed by critics as the show's greatest performance to date.

The glee club kids dressed up in renditions of Gaga's most notorious costumes, including Gaga's bubble outfit and a dress made from Beanie Babies stuffed toys, a nod to her Kermit the Frog outfit. The show's one gay character, Kurt, wore a bizarre space-age silver dress, tights, and a version of the lobster-claw shoes that Gaga often wears. Other highlights of the episode included an acoustic version of "Poker Face" by the lead character Rachel and her mother. Gaga praised the episode on Twitter and has come out as a fan of the show. After the episode aired,

Cast members on the TV show Glee perform popular cover songs in each episode, including "Bad Romance," by Lady Gaga.

Gaga posted on Twitter, "GLEE WAS SO AMAZING! AH!!!!"[51] The cast of *Glee* was also pleased and cited "Bad Romance" and the Gaga episode in general when asked about their favorite moments from the show at Comic-Con International in July 2010.

The Queen of Pop Culture

Lady Gaga's connections with other enterprises, her outrageous fashion choices, self-important—and often untrue—statements during interviews, and controversial antics (both on and off the stage) keep her name in the news. As long as she makes headlines, she stays relevant and is thus able to influence culture. AlterNet contributor Sarah Jaffe has put Gaga's domination of pop culture in the following way: "Lady Gaga launched a full-on assault on the culture and scrambled her way to the top, planted a designer six-inch heel and raised her flag."[52] Indeed, Lady Gaga's biggest talent may not be her voice but rather her ability to manipulate the media in order to exert her influence and maintain her ultra-famous status.

Chapter 6

Gaga's Causes

Lady Gaga is passionate about human rights and uses her celebrity to support the causes she cares most about. Gaga's charitable pursuits and commitment to her disenfranchised fans inspires her to keep writing music so that she can lend her influential voice to those who need a spokesperson.

Gaga for Gays

Like Madonna in the 1980s and 1990s, Gaga mixes entertainment with politics, particularly gay rights. Gaga uses her star power to speak out against what she views as injustices toward the gay community. And in turn, Lady Gaga's music, style, and outspoken dedication to gay rights have made her an icon for the current generation of gay, lesbian, bisexual, and transgender Americans.

Gaga, who sometimes self-identifies as bisexual, has made it a priority to mainstream homosexuality. As she puts it, "I very much want to inject gay culture into the mainstream. It's not an underground tool for me. It's my whole life. So I always sort of joke the real motivation is to just turn the world gay."[53] She invites Americans to reject social norms and let their true selves emerge—even if only at her concerts. She often announces at her shows that the "freaks" are outside the doors of the venue and that all of her Little Monsters are safe and loved and free to express themselves. She has been both lauded by fans and accused by critics of promoting a gay agenda through her music.

Her songs and videos often carry homosexual themes and undertones. For example, Gaga has said that her megahit "Poker Face" is about a woman who fantasizes about being with another woman while she is being intimate with a man. The video for "Telephone" features transgender and transsexual women,

Lady Gaga hugs former gay members of the military at a rally. Gaga is fighting for gays to have equal rights with other Americans.

and Gaga kisses a woman in the opening sequence. Gaga has also stated that the video for "Alejandro" was inspired by her love for her gay friends and fans. These songs have become akin to gay anthems that can be heard anywhere there is music and are frequently played in dance clubs, fitness centers, and supermarkets.

"Mother Monster," as Gaga is affectionately called by her fans, has a very public love affair with her gay fans. She often thanks God as well as gays when she wins awards and repeatedly credits her gay fan base in interviews for her success. Before Gaga was selling out major concert venues, she played gay clubs in New York City. She reminds anyone with whom she partners that if they get on board with Lady Gaga, they must be willing to get on board with gay culture. For example, when she and rapper Kanye West were considering touring together, she told him, "I'm gay. My music is gay. My show is gay. And I *love* that it's gay. And I love my gay fans and they're all going to be coming to our show. And it's going to *remain* gay."[54] *Out* magazine went so far as to declare that gayness was part of the "Gagaland constitution."[55]

This constitution does not just cover the superficial aspects of gay culture, however. Lady Gaga is also a staunch believer that gays are entitled to the rights and privileges afforded to the heterosexual majority. Through her, they have a voice in mainstream culture, and she uses it to further two causes she feels passionately about: the right to marry and the right to serve openly in the military.

Gay Marriage

Lady Gaga passionately believes gay couples should be afforded the right to marry, and she uses public appearances as opportunities to speak out in favor of gay marriage. In October 2009, Lady Gaga was invited to speak and perform at the Human Rights Campaign Dinner in Washington, D.C. President Barack Obama was also in attendance, and he opened his remarks by acknowledging Gaga's megastar status. "It is a privilege to be here tonight to open for Lady Gaga,"[56] he joked, and the crowd

Is Gaga Gay?

Lady Gaga is often coy about her sexual orientation, though she has stated that the song "Poker Face" is a metaphor for bisexuality. She told Barbara Walters in a 2009 interview that she has never been in love with a woman but has been intimate with women. She has also said, "I myself am not a gay woman—I am a free spirited woman." Speculation about Gaga's ambiguous sexuality even led to rumors that she was a hermaphrodite or transsexual. She has stated to journalists during interviews that both are untrue, yet curious fans and spiteful critics still wonder. Given the rigorous demands of her touring, performing, and recording schedules, she has indicated that she does not have time to meet anyone—male or female—who might prove to be a romantic interest for her.

Quoted in Joshua David Stein and Noah Michelson, "The Lady Is a Vamp," *Out,* September 2009. www.out.com/exclusives.asp?id=25701.

Despite rumors, Lady Gaga has stated in interviews that she is "not a gay woman—I am a free spirited woman."

Gaga has been outspoken about the need to repeal DADT, as it discriminates against her favorite population. Fans and critics have articulated that Gaga's video for "Alejandro" was meant to be a commentary on "Don't Ask, Don't Tell." The video features militaristic dancers scantily clad in little more than black underwear. The men wear heels. They march in unison and perform homoerotic dances as Gaga watches from a throne.

Gaga showed her commitment to ending the ban on openly gay soldiers serving in the military when she brought four gay veterans as her dates to the 2010 *MTV Video Music Awards*. In a symbolic gesture, Gaga donned a dress and shoes made entirely of raw meat. She also carried a meat purse crusted with jewels and wore a slab of meat on her head as a hat. She told Ellen DeGeneres in a September 13, 2010, interview that the dress symbolized oppression. She said to DeGeneres, "If we don't stand up for what we believe in and if we don't fight for our rights, pretty soon we're going to have as much rights as the meat on our own bones."[60]

Gaga also Tweeted a message to ask Senate Majority Leader Harry Reid to call for a vote in the Senate to repeal DADT. She also posted a nearly eight-minute-long video on her website in which she called on members of the Senate to vote to debate a defense spending bill that included language that would overturn DADT. Gaga also joined a rally in Portland, Maine, on September 20, 2010, where two thousand protestors gathered to call on the state's two moderate Republican senators to vote to repeal DADT. In December 2010 the "Don't Ask, Don't Tell Repeal Act of 2010" passed in both the House and Senate. The Act was signed into law by President Barack Obama on December 22, 2010, though it does not take effect immediately.

It is interesting to note that although Gaga purports to want to normalize homosexuality, critics in the gay community have charged that her videos actually portray homosexuality as overly sexualized and deviant. They argue that she does not forward gay causes when she mixes blasphemous religious themes and murder with homosexuality, such as in the controversial "Telephone" video. Despite these points, Lady Gaga has made working on behalf of gay rights issues a central part of her identity and celebrity.

A Charitable Lady

In addition to gay rights, Lady Gaga is also committed to several other causes and charities. For example, Gaga partnered with Virgin Mobile, her tour sponsor, during *The Monster Ball* tour to help homeless youth. Gaga pledged to match every dollar that was donated (up to twenty-five thousand dollars) to Virgin Mobile's Re*Generation program. In addition, Gaga and Virgin Mobile together offered VIP tickets to fans who volunteered with homeless youth organizations. The special ticket packages included a souvenir, special seating, and even the chance to meet Gaga. The endeavor raised more than eighty thousand dollars and generated thirty thousand hours of community service for hundreds of different homeless youth organizations across the country.

In January 2010, Lady Gaga took the opportunity to discuss another charitable venture during an interview with talk-show host Oprah Winfrey. Gaga begged viewers to help victims in Haiti who suffered the catastrophic 7.0 earthquake that killed

Lady Gaga's Celebrity Fans

Lady Gaga's throng of fans, her Little Monsters, is a diverse bunch. She even counts many celebrities among some of her biggest fans. Jay-Z and Beyoncé Knowles are both admirers, to the point that Beyoncé collaborated with Gaga on the single "Telephone." Elton John and Lady Gaga share a mutual admiration, and the two opened the 2010 Grammy Awards with a duet. Cyndi Lauper was an early and ardent Gaga supporter, and the two do charity work together. Even Michael Jackson was rumored to be a Gaga fan before his death in 2009. Gaga revealed to Larry King that Jackson wanted her to open for him on his *This Is It* tour and even wanted to do duets onstage.

more than 230,000 people on January 12, 2010. The earthquake left more than 1 million people homeless and leveled more than a quarter of a million private homes and commercial buildings.

Gaga announced on *The Oprah Winfrey Show*, Twitter, Facebook, and her website that 100 percent of the proceeds from ticket and merchandise sales from her January 24, 2010, concert at Radio City Music Hall would be donated to the earthquake relief fund. In addition, all of the proceeds from merchandise sold on Gaga's website on "Gaga for Haiti" day (also January 24, 2010) was donated to quake victims. The effort raised more than five hundred thousand dollars in one day.

VIVA Glam

In addition to her other charity work, Lady Gaga is the spokesperson (alongside pop star Cyndi Lauper) for the VIVA Glam campaign against AIDS and HIV. The campaign is a project of the MAC AIDS Fund—MAC is a high-end makeup company that sells VIVA Glam lipstick and "lipglass." All proceeds from the VIVA Glam lip line fund the MAC AIDS Fund. The fund provides money to help mostly women and children, but also men, who have AIDS or who are HIV positive.

The campaign has raised more than $150 million and is a cause that is close to Gaga's heart. Gaga said of the campaign, "We want women to feel strong . . . enough that they can remember to protect themselves. To have this lipstick as a reminder in your purse. . . you put your lipstick on, and you bring a condom out with you."[61]

Gaga, like her VIVA Glam spokesperson predecessors, Boy George, RuPaul, and Lil' Kim, has her own colors in the VIVA Glam lip line. She is featured in ads for the product and promotes the campaign in interviews and on her website. Monies from the sale of the lipsticks provide education and services to people affected by HIV and AIDS. Some of the services provided by the proceeds include counseling sessions for HIV-positive women, child care during doctor's appointments, boxes of non-

Connecting with Gay Youth Through *Glee*

Gaga's connection to gay youth was highlighted in the Gaga episode of *Glee,* which was appropriately titled "Theatricality." The girls and Kurt, the show's gay character, explored their individuality through their choice of Gaga songs and costumes. The boys in the glee club were uncomfortable doing Gaga, so instead they performed songs by Kiss (a popular rock band from the 1970s that dressed in costumes during performances). The episode incorporated themes from Gaga's songs, videos, and politics. These included the need to stand up against homophobia, the right to be different from the mainstream majority, and the bias and abuse inflicted against the gay community. In the episode, Kurt epitomizes Gaga's message when he says, "I'm proud to be different. It's the best thing about me."

Quoted in *Glee,* "Theatricality," Fox, May 25, 2010. www.fox.com/watch/glee.

perishable food, transportation for a month for women with HIV/AIDS to get to doctor's appointments, school supplies for kids orphaned by HIV/AIDS, and nutritional counseling for patients with HIV/AIDS.

Here to Stay

There is every indication that Lady Gaga's extensive charitable endeavors, media savvy, commitment to her army of Little Monsters, elaborately executed performances, and commitment to celebrity means that she is building momentum toward a long-lasting career. Indeed, the megastar has come a long way since her Lollapalooza appearance with Lady Starlight on a small side stage in Chicago's Grant Park in 2007.

In August 2010, Lady Gaga returned to Grant Park to perform at Lollapalooza. This time, however, she was a headliner. She brought her huge stage production with her. Perry Farrell, creator of the three-day festival that brought in about ninety thousand people per day, said that Gaga's stage cost about $150,000 to build. He added that Gaga was a natural fit for the lineup: "I so appreciate someone who brings show. I mean, I'm building things just waiting for people like her. It's just natural. For Lollapalooza you've got the Chicago skyline and Lady Gaga. There it is."[62]

Like Farrell, Gaga's fans, critics, and celebrity peers cannot help but recognize her commitment to show business. It is apparent in everything she does, which makes Lady Gaga a true entertainer who is never out of character. She has said she models her persona after the late and eccentric entertainer Michael Jackson. She said, "If I were to ever, God forbid, get hurt onstage and my fans were screaming outside of the hospital, waiting for me to come out, I'd come out as Gaga. Michael [Jackson] got burned, and he lifted that glittered glove so damn high so his fans could see him, because he was in the art of show business. That's what we do."[63]

Lady Gaga's third album, *Born This Way*, was scheduled to be released in the spring of 2011, and Gaga claims that her fans will not be disappointed. Indeed, with Lady Gaga providing an endless supply of new songs, inventions, tricks, and a nearly nonstop tour schedule, it is clear her Little Monsters will have plenty to look forward to from their Mother Monster.

![Notes]

Introduction: A Glorious Reality Based on Beautiful Lies

1. Quoted in "Lady Gaga Stops Show to Break Up a Fight in Washington D.C. Concert Monster," YouTube, September 7, 2010. www.youtube.com/watch?v=SbeRqfV9I24&feature=related.
2. Quoted in "Manifesto of Little Monsters," YouTube. www.youtube.com/watch?v=Nikc3OUj3qo.
3. Quoted in Brian Hiatt, "The Rise of Lady Gaga," *Rolling Stone*, June 11, 2009.
4. Jon Caramanica, "The Truth Behind Lady Gaga: A Distraction as an End in Itself," *Vancouver (BC) Sun*, August 23, 2010. www.vancouversun.com/entertainment/truth+behind+Lady+Gaga+distraction+itself/3433447/story.html.
5. Quoted in *Ok!*, "Celebrities Should Never Look Casual," March 30, 2010. www.ok.co.uk/celebnews/view/20168/Lady-GaGa-interview-Celebrities-should-never-look-casual.
6. Rick Newman, "How Lady Gaga Embodies America's Prosperity Trap," *U.S. News & World Report*, August 20, 2010. http://money.usnews.com/money/blogs/flowchart/2010/8/20/how-lady-gaga-embodies-americas-prosperity-trap.

Chapter 1: Life Before Gaga

7. Quoted in Vanessa Grigoriadis, "Growing Up Gaga," *New York*, March 28, 2010. http://nymag.com/arts/popmusic/features/65127.
8. Quoted in Grigoriadis, "Growing Up Gaga."
9. Quoted in "Ellen Gets the Details from Lady Gaga," *The Ellen Degeneres Show*, November 27, 2009. http://ellen.warnerbros.com/2009/11/lady-gaga-details-1127.php.
10. Quoted in Neil McCormack, "Lady Gaga: 'I've Always Been Famous and You Just Didn't Know It,'" *Telegraph*, February

16, 2010. www.telegraph.co.uk/culture/music/rockandpop features/7221051/Lady-Gaga-Ive-always-been-famous-you-just-didnt-know-it.html.

11. Lady Gaga's Official Website, "Biography." www.ladygaga .com/bio.

12. Quoted in Webjockey Spiceboyedgar, "Lady Gaga," *Riffin'*, July 2008. www.riffin.com/iframes/record/artist_spot lights/Lady_Gaga.html.

13. Quoted in John Seabrook, "Transformer," *New Yorker*, February 1, 2010. www.newyorker.com/talk/2010/02/01/ 100201ta_talk_seabrook.

Chapter 2: The Emergence of Lady Gaga

14. Quoted in Craig Marks, "Producer Rob Fusari Dishes on Lady Gaga, Beyoncé," *Billboard*, February 24, 2010. www .billboard.com/features/producer-rob-fusari-dishes-on-lady-gaga-1004070301.story#/features/producer-rob-fusari-dishes-on-lady-gaga-1004070301.story?page=1.

15. Quoted in Lisa Rose, "Lady Gaga's Outrageous Persona Born in Parsippany, New Jersey," *Newark (NJ) Star Ledger*, January 21, 2010. www.nj.com/entertainment/music/index .ssf/2010/01/lady_gaga_her_outrageous_perso.html.

16. Quoted in DJ Ron Slomowicz, "Interview with Lady Gaga," About.com, June 10, 2008. http://dancemusic.about.com/ od/artistshomepages/a/LadyGagaInt_2.htm.

17. Brendan Sullivan, "Lady Gaga: The Grandmother of Pop," *Esquire*, April 26, 2010. www.esquire.com/women/women-issue/lady-gaga-bio-and-pics-0510.

18. Quoted in Sullivan, "Lady Gaga."

19. Quoted in Emily Herbert, *Lady Gaga: Behind the Fame.* New York: Overlook, 2010, p. 35.

20. Quoted in Cortney Harding, "Lady Gaga: The Billboard Cover Story," *Billboard*, August 7, 2009. www.billboard.com/ features/lady-gaga-the-billboard-cover-story-1004001347 .story?page=2#/features/lady-gaga-the-billboard-cover-story-1004001347.story?page=3.

21. Quoted in Ryan Pearson, "Akon: Lady Gaga Made Me Rich," *Huffington Post,* February 17, 2010. www.huffingtonpost

.com/2010/02/17/akon-lady-gaga-made-me-ri_n_465641
.html.

22. Quoted in Chris Harris, with reporting by Kim Stolz, "Lady Gaga Brings Her Artistic Vision of Pop Music to New Album—and a 'New Kids' Song," MTV News, June 9, 2008. www.mtv.com/news/articles/1589013/20080609/lady_gaga.jhtml.

23. Quoted in Harding, "Lady Gaga."

Chapter 3: The Year of Gaga

24. Jill Menze, "Lady Gaga/May 2, 2009/New York/(Terminal 5)," *Billboard*, May 4, 2009. www.billboard.com/bbcom/reviews-live/lady-gaga-may-2-2009-new-york-terminal-5-1003969033.story#/bbcom/reviews-live/lady-gaga-may-2-2009-new-york-terminal-5-1003969033.story.

25. Quoted in Seabrook, "Transformer."

26. Gil Kaufman, "Lady Gaga Shows Her Flashiest 'Poker Face' on *American Idol*," MTV News, April 2, 2009. www.mtv.com/news/articles/1608347/20090402/lady_gaga.jhtml.

27. David Drake, "Top 100 Tracks of 2009," Pitchfork, December 14, 2009. http://pitchfork.com/features/staff-lists/7742-the-top-100-tracks-of-2009/7.

28. Lady Gaga, Twitter, February 2, 2010. http://twitter.com/ladygaga/status/8561296471.

29. Sal Cinquemani, "Lady Gaga: The Fame," *Slant*, October 25, 2008. www.slantmagazine.com/music/review/lady-gaga-the-fame/1545.

30. Cinquemani, "Lady Gaga."

31. J. Freedom du Lac, "'Fame' Isn't Worth Getting Gaga Over," *Washington Post*, October 28, 2008. www.washingtonpost.com/wp-dyn/content/article/2008/10/27/AR2008102702579.html.

32. Chris Riemenschneider, "Lady Gaga Is a Phone-y," *Minneapolis Star-Tribune*, August 31, 2010. www.startribune.com/entertainment/music/101607498.html?elr=KArksD:aDyaEP:kD:aUnOiP3UiacyKUnciaec8O7EyUr.

33. Quoted in Simon Hattenstone, "Grace Jones: 'God I'm Scary; I'm Scaring Myself,'" *Guardian*, April 17, 2010. www.guardian.co.uk/music/2010/apr/17/grace-jones-interview.

34. Quoted in NME, "MIA: 'Lady Gaga Is a Mimic,'" April 9, 2010. www.nme.com/news/mia/50571.

Chapter 4: Designing Gaga

35. Quoted in Sarah Deeks, "Armani Goes Gaga," *Vogue*, May 6, 2010. www.vogue.co.uk/news/daily/100506-lady-gagas-style-by-giorgio-armani.aspx.
36. Amber Jones, "The Lady Gaga and Alexander McQueen Connection," PopEater, February 11, 2010. www.popeater.com/2010/02/11/alexander-mcqueen-lady-gaga.
37. Quoted in Rachel Dodes, "Lady Gaga Was Alexander Mc-Queen's 'Unofficial Muse,'" *Wall Street Journal*, February 11, 2010. http://blogs.wsj.com/runway/2010/02/11/lady-gaga-was-mcqueens-unofficial-muse.
38. Quoted in Chris Harris and Kim Stolz, "Lady Gaga Brings Her Artistic Vision of Pop to New Album," MTV News, June 9, 2008. www.mtv.com/news/articles/1589013/20080609/lady_gaga.jhtml.
39. Quoted in Jocelyn Vena and Sway Calloway, "Lady Gaga Plans to Battle Her 'Monsters' During Monster Ball Tour," MTV News, November 6, 2009. www.mtv.com/news/articles/1625651/20091105/lady_gaga.jhtml.
40. Quoted in Sway, "Lady Gaga's Monster Ball Tour: The Concept," MTV News. www.mtv.com/videos/news/453125/lady-gagas-monster-ball-tour-the-concept.jhtml#id=1625515.
41. Ryan White, "Concert Review: Lady Gaga Invites Us All to the Rose Garden for the Monster Ball," *Oregonian*, August 20, 2010. www.oregonlive.com/music/index.ssf/2010/08/live_review_lady_gaga_invites.html.
42. Joe Brown, "Mutant Showgirl: Lady Gaga Touches Down in Las Vegas," *Las Vegas Sun*, December 18, 2009. www.lasvegassun.com/news/2009/dec/18/mutant-showgirl-lady-gaga-touches-down-las-vegas.
43. Quoted in Grigoriadis, "Growing Up Gaga."
44. Grigoriadis, "Growing Up Gaga."
45. Lisa Robinson, "Lady Gaga's Cultural Revolution," *Vanity Fair*, September 2010, p. 282.

46. Quoted in Lisa O'Neill, "Lady Gaga's Frog Fetish: Singer Wears Kermit the Frog Coat, Laden with Dozens of the Muppet," *New York Daily News*, July 21, 2009. www.nydailynews.com/lifestyle/fashion/2009/07/21/2009-07-21_lady_gagas_frog_fetish_singer_wears_kermit_the_frog_coat_laden_with_dozens_of_th.html.

Chapter 5: Media Domination, Cultural Sensation

47. Sam Machkovech, "Beyond Gaga: Two Trailblazing Female Singers," *Atlantic*, June 10, 2010. www.theatlantic.com/culture/archive/2010/06/beyond-gaga-two-trailblazing-female-singers/57918.
48. Quoted in Ryan, Monty, and Wippa, "Lady Gaga Chats to Her 'Little Monsters,'" Nova 96.9 FM, March 23, 2010. www.novafm.com.au/Audio.aspx?id=96892&site=Nova969&s=78.
49. Quoted in Vanessa Grigoriadis, "Sex, God, and Katy Perry," *Rolling Stone*, August 19, 2010. www.rollingstone.com/music/news/17386/188135.
50. Quoted in "Jerry Seinfeld Calls Out Lady Gaga for Her Foul Temper," *New York Post*, June 22, 2010. www.nypost.com/p/news/local/jerry_seinfeld_calls_calls_lady_1bVWKP67rYxAPhn3qEbGvI.
51. Lady Gaga, Twitter, May 26, 2010. http://twitter.com/ladygaga/status/14770658739.
52. Sarah Jaffe, "Lady Gaga: Pop Star for a Country and an Empire in Decline," AlterNet, July 26, 2010. www.alternet.org/media/147625/lady_gaga%3A_pop_star_for_a_country_and_an_empire_in_decline.

Chapter 6: Gaga's Causes

53. Quoted in Joshua David Stein and Noah Michelson, "The Lady Is a Vamp," *Out*, September 2009. www.out.com/exclusives.asp?id=25701.
54. Quoted in Stein and Michelson, "The Lady Is a Vamp."
55. Stein and Michelson, "The Lady Is a Vamp."

56. Barack Obama, "Remarks by the President at Human Rights Campaign Dinner," White House, October 11, 2009. www .whitehouse.gov/the-press-office/remarks-president-human-rights-campaign-dinner.

57. Quoted in Michael Solis, "Lady Gaga and Obama for Gay America," *Huffington Post,* August 22, 2010. www.huffing tonpost.com/michael-solis/lady-gaga-and-obama-for-g_b_318088.html.

58. Lady Gaga, Twitter, August 4, 2010. http://twitter.com/ladygaga/status/20350379949.

59. Quoted in Ryan Seacrest, "Lady Gaga Explains Going Crowd Surfing at Lollapalooza," RyanSeacrest.com, August 11, 2010. www.ryanseacrest.com/blog/whats-happening/lady-gaga-explains-going-crowd-surfing-at-lollapalooza-audio.

60. Quoted in "Lady Gaga Is Victorious at the VMAs!" *The Ellen DeGeneres Show*, September 13, 2010. http://ellen.warner bros.com/2010/09/lady_gaga_is_victorious_at_the_vmas_vod_0913.php.

61. Quoted in James Montgomery and Garth Bardsley, "Lady Gaga, Cyndi Lauper Raise AIDS Awareness with Lipstick," MTV News, February 10, 2010. www.mtv.com/news/articles/1631673/20100210/lady_gaga.jhtml.

62. Quoted in Angela Watercutter, "Perry Farrell: Lady Gaga Was My Lollapalooza Marble," *Wired*, June 8, 2010. www .wired.com/underwire/2010/06/perry-farrell-lollapalooza.

63. Quoted in Neil Strauss, "The Broken Heart and Violent Fantasies of Lady Gaga," *Rolling Stone*, July 8–22, 2010, p. 70.

1986
Stefani Joanne Angelina Germanotta is born on March 28 to Joseph and Cynthia Germanotta.

1990
Germanotta learns to play the piano by ear when she is just four years old.

1992
Gaga plays her first piano recital at the exclusive Convent of the Sacred Heart Academy in Manhattan.

1999
Writes her first piano ballad, "To Love Again."

2001
The September 11, 2001, attacks on New York and Washington leave a lasting impression on the fifteen-year-old.

2002
Records her first demo.

2003
Is one of only twenty students admitted that year to the prestigious Tisch School of the Arts at New York University.

2005
Drops out of Tisch to begin pursuing a music career full-time. Begins performing with the SGBand (Stefani Germanotta Band).

2006
Singer and talent scout Wendy Starland sees the SGBand perform and introduces Germanotta to producer Rob Fusari. The two begin working on songs together.

Changes her name to Lady Gaga, a play on the Queen song "Radio Ga Ga." Insists on being called Lady Gaga from that point forward.

Is briefly signed to Def Jam Recordings but is quickly dropped. She gets a contract shortly thereafter with Interscope Records.

Gaga meets Lady Starlight in March.

Signs a music publishing deal with Sony/ATV Music Publishing. She will eventually write songs for Britney Spears, New Kids on the Block, and the Pussycat Dolls.

2007

Gaga and Lady Starlight begin performing as *Lady Gaga and the Starlight Revue*. Their performances gain them some notoriety, and they play Chicago's Lollapalooza music festival in August. Gaga's performance receives mostly positive reviews.

Sings a guide vocal for producer/performer Akon. He recognizes her potential and obtains permission from Interscope to sign Gaga to his label, Kon Live Distribution.

2008

Records *The Fame* quickly early in the year. The first single, "Just Dance," is released on April 8. It becomes an instant dance club anthem. The full album is released on August 19. To promote the album, Gaga makes appearances on *So You Think You Can Dance*, *Jimmy Kimmel Live!*, *The Tonight Show with Jay Leno*, and other television shows. She also performs as the opening act for label mates New Kids on the Block during their 2008 tour.

2009

Kicks off her first solo world tour, *The Fame Ball*, at the House of Blues in San Diego on March 12. The tour lasts for six months and comprises seventy shows played throughout North America, Asia, and Europe.

In July, surpasses Barack Obama as the person with the most friends on Facebook (more than 10 million fans).

Begins her television media blitz: performs on an *American Idol* elimination episode in April; performs on the *Ellen DeGeneres Show* and *Dancing with the Stars* in May; is the musical guest on the Ryan Reynolds episode of *Saturday Night Live* in October (performs in a sketch with Madonna); appears on the *Gossip Girl* episode "The Last Days of Disco Stick" in November.

Speaks and performs at the Human Rights Campaign dinner in Washington, D.C., on October 10.

The Fame Monster, an eight-track EP of entirely new Gaga material, is released on November 18.

Announces *The Monster Ball* tour in October 2009 to replace the canceled *Fame Kills* tour she was to coheadline with Kanye West. *The Monster Ball* tour begins on November 27 in Montreal, Canada.

Gives a memorable performance of "Paparazzi" at the 2009 *MTV Video Music Awards* and wins an award for Best New Artist. "Paparazzi" wins awards for Best Art Direction and Best Special Effects. Gaga also performs at the *American Music Awards* and the Grammy Nominations Concert. Performs for Queen Elizabeth II at the Royal Variety Performance in December. Is named one of the "Ten Most Fascinating People of 2009" by Barbara Walters.

2010

Gaga must reschedule a show at Purdue when she passes out backstage in January. She goes on *The Oprah Winfrey Show* and apologizes to fans.

Alexander McQueen, who designed many outfits for Gaga, commits suicide in February. Gaga dedicates her BRIT Awards performance to him.

Nearly faints onstage at a show in New Zealand in March. This, combined with the January fainting at Purdue, leads to rumors that Gaga may be ill, perhaps with the autoimmune condition lupus.

The video for her single "Telephone," featuring Beyoncé Knowles, is released. It is set in an all-female prison. Bill O'Reilly, the conservative pundit and Gaga detractor, airs a clip of the video in his show and is criticized by other conservatives for promoting her.

Is named one of *Time* magazine's "100 Most Influential People of the Year" in April.

In May, performs for a second time on *American Idol*. An entire episode of *Glee* is dedicated to her music and style.

Is interviewed by Larry King in June. Answers the lupus rumors, stating that she does not have the condition but is at risk for developing it and that her aunt died of lupus.

The video for "Alejandro" is released on June 8. It is widely discussed and criticized for its juxtaposition of religious, fascist, and gay imagery. Also in June, Gaga receives some negative press after attending a Mets game and making an obscene gesture at paparazzi. Later the same month, she also goes to a Yankees game and is permanently banned from the team's clubhouse after she sneaks in following the game.

In August, is nominated for a record thirteen *MTV Video Music Awards* for the "Bad Romance" and "Telephone" videos; returns to Lollapalooza, this time as a headliner.

In September, wins eight *MTV Video Music Awards*, including Video of the Year for "Bad Romance." Is the keynote speaker at a rally to repeal the Don't Ask, Don't Tell policy in Portland, Maine.

Books

Jack Bankowsky, Alison M. Gingeras, and Catherine Wood, eds., *Pop Life: Art in a Material World*. London: Tate, 2009. A collection of prints and essays on pop art, a movement that heavily influenced Lady Gaga.

Elizabeth Goodman, *Lady Gaga: Critical Mass Fashion*. New York: St. Martin's Griffin, 2010. This book catalogs Lady Gaga's outrageous fashions, showcasing the creations of the Haus of Gaga as well as the designs of Alexander McQueen and other fashion masters.

Emily Herbert, *Lady Gaga: Behind the Fame*. New York: Overlook, 2010. This book presents an overview of Gaga's life from her childhood up to the release of *The Fame Monster*.

Helia Phoenix, *Lady Gaga—Just Dance: The Biography*. London: Orion, 2010. An unauthorized biography on the life of Lady Gaga by rock journalist Helia Phoenix. Upon its release, the book was cited in tabloids for Gaga's quotes regarding drug use and the nature of her sexuality.

Andy Warhol, *The Philosophy of Andy Warhol: From A to B and Back Again*. San Diego: Harcourt, 1975. A compendium of musings on various topics like love, death, success, art, and fame by one of Gaga's main inspirations and a huge figure in the world of pop art.

Periodicals

Nandini D'Souza, "Going Ga-Ga for Lady Gaga," *W*, October 2007.

Sasha Frere-Jones, "Ladies Wild: How Not Dumb Is Gaga?" *New Yorker*, April 27, 2009.

Vanessa Grigoriadis, "Growing Up Gaga," *New York*, March 28, 2010.

Cortney Harding, "Lady Gaga: The Billboard Cover Story," *Billboard*, August 7, 2009.

Brian Hiatt, "The Rise of Lady Gaga," *Rolling Stone*, May 30, 2009.

Lisa Robinson, "Lady Gaga's Cultural Revolution," *Vanity Fair*, September 2010.

Christine Spines, "Lady Gaga Wants You," *Cosmopolitan*, April 2010.

Joshua David Stein and Noah Michelson, "The Lady Is a Vamp," *Out*, September 2009.

Neil Strauss, "The Broken Heart and Violent Fantasies of Lady Gaga," *Rolling Stone*, July 8–22, 2010.

Brendan Sullivan, "Lady Gaga: The Grandmother of Pop," *Esquire*, April 26, 2010.

Joe Zee, "Lady Gaga—an Exclusive Interview with ELLE's January Cover Girl," *Elle*, December 1, 2009.

Internet Sources

ArtistDirect, "Interview: Lady Gaga," January 30, 2009. www .artistdirect.com/nad/news/article/0,,4931544,00.html.

Maureen Callahan and Sarah Stewart, "Who's That Lady?" *New York Post*, January 2010. www.nypost.com/p/entertainment/ music/who_that_lady_CBlHI927dRlLmIwjVfGrwK.

Margaret Eby, "Get Your Ph.D. in Lady Gaga," Salon, May 2010. www.salon.com/life/broadsheet/2010/05/28/lady_gaga_ academic_journal.

Cyndi Lauper, "Lady Gaga: The 2010 TIME 100," *Time*, April 29, 2010. www.time.com/time/specials/packages/ article/0,28804,1984685_1984940_1984943,00.html.

Los Angeles Times, "Lady Gaga by the Numbers," August 11, 2010. http://articles.latimes.com/2010/aug/11/entertainment/ la-et-lady-gaga-stats-20100811.

Oscar Moralde, "Pop Ate My Heart: Lady Gaga, Her Videos, and Her Fame Monster," *Slant*, December 14, 2009. www.slant magazine.com/house/2009/12/pop-ate-my-heart-lady-gaga- her-videos-and-her-fame-monster.

Lisa Rose, "Lady Gaga's Outrageous Persona Born in Parsippany, New Jersey," *Newark (NJ) Star-Ledger*, January 2010. www

.nj.com/entertainment/music/index.ssf/2010/01/lady_gaga_
her_outrageous_perso.html.

Fiona Sturges, "Lady Gaga: How the World Went Crazy for the New Queen of Pop," *Independent*, May 2009. www.indepen dent.co.uk/arts-entertainment/music/features/lady-gaga-how-the-world-went-crazy-for-the-new-queen-of-pop-1684375 .html.

Jonah Weiner, "How Smart Is Lady Gaga?" *Slate,* June 16, 2009. www.slate.com/id/2220502.

Dan Zak, "For Gay Activists, the Lady Is a Champ," *Washington Post*, October 12, 2009. www.washingtonpost.com/wp-dyn/ content/article/2009/10/11/AR2009101101892.html?hpid=t opnews&sid=ST2009101101924.

Websites

Gaga Stigmata (http://gagajournal.blogspot.com). An online journal dedicated to the serious study of Lady Gaga as a genuine cultural phenomenon. The site is a compendium of essays and artwork.

Lady Gaga (www.ladygaga.com). The official place on the web for all things Gaga. Includes a biography, videos, discography, fan forums, and much more.

Lady Gaga on Interscope Records (www.interscope.com/lady gaga). Information about official releases, remixes, and various media projects.

Picture Credits

Cover: Steve Granitz/Wire Image/Getty Images
AP Images/Ali Paige Goldstein, 32
AP Images/Amanda Schwab, 79
AP Images/Charles Sykes, 26
AP Images/Eduardo Verdugo, 17
AP Images/Evan Agostini, 63
AP Images/Lady Gaga The Monster Ball Tour, 38
AP Images/Matt Sayles, 43
AP Images/Pat Wellenbach, 81
AP Images/Peter Kramer, 8, 45
AP Images/Robert Scheer, 64
AP Images/Scott Gries, 40
Barry King/WireImage/Getty Images, 58
Cory Schwartz/Getty Images, 19
Daniel Boczarkski/Getty Images, 29
David Livingston/Getty Images, 22
Dimitrios Kambouris/Wire Image/Getty Images, 48
Fox TV/The Kobal Collection/The Picture Desk, Inc., 74
Jason Merritt/Getty Images, 60
Jeff Kravitz/FilmMagic/Getty Images, 53
Joel Page/Reuters/Landov, 77
John Angilillo/UPI/Landov, 69
John Medina/WireImage/Getty Images, 30
Kevin Mazur/WireImage/Getty Images, 15
Larry Busacca/Getty Images, 11
Leon Neal/PA Photos/Landov, 51
Roger Kisby/Getty Images, 66
Roger Williams/UPI/Landov, 36
Stephen Lovekin/WireImage/Getty Images, 55

About the Author

Claire Kreger-Boaz is a writer who lives in San Diego, California. She has written several books and articles, including music reviews. Claire lives with her three favorite "Little Monsters," John, Max, and Ruby, without whom she would get a lot more done but have much less fun.